PERGAMON INTERNATIONAL LIBRARY
of Science, Technology, Engineering and Social Studies

*The 1000-volume original paperback library in aid of education,
industrial training and the enjoyment of leisure*

Publisher: Robert Maxwell, M.C.

EATING DISORDERS

PS. 6

D 7-Graph

D1117026

THE PERGAMON TEXTBOOK
INSPECTION COPY SERVICE

An inspection copy of any book published in the Pergamon International Library
will gladly be sent to academic staff without obligation for their consideration for
course adoption or recommendation. Copies may be retained for a period of 60 days
from receipt and returned if not suitable. When a particular title is adopted or
recommended for adoption for class use and the recommendation results in a sale
of 12 or more copies the inspection copy may be retained with our compliments.
The Publishers will be pleased to receive suggestions for revised editions and new
titles to be published in this important international Library.

Pergamon Titles of Related Interest

Blanchard / Andrasik MANAGEMENT OF CHRONIC HEADACHES:
A Psychological Approach

Holzman / Turk PAIN MANAGEMENT: A Handbook of Psychological
Treatment Approaches

Kirschenbaum / Johnson / Stalonas TREATING CHILDHOOD AND
ADOLESCENT OBESITY

Weiss / Katzman / Wolchik TREATING BULIMIA:
A Psychoeducational Approach

Related Journals
(Free sample copies available upon request)

CLINICAL PSYCHOLOGY REVIEW
SOCIAL SCIENCES AND MEDICINE

PSYCHOLOGY PRACTITIONER GUIDEBOOKS

EDITORS
Arnold P. Goldstein, Syracuse University
Leonard Krasner, Stanford University and SUNY at Stony Brook
Sol L. Garfield, Washington University

EATING DISORDERS
Management of Obesity, Bulimia, and Anorexia Nervosa

W. STEWART AGRAS
Stanford University School of Medicine

PERGAMON PRESS
New York   Oxford   Beijing   Frankfurt   São Paulo   Sydney   Tokyo   Toronto

Pergamon Press Offices:

U.S.A.	Pergamon Press, Maxwell House, Fairview Park, Elmsford, New York 10523, U.S.A.
U.K.	Pergamon Press, Headington Hill Hall, Oxford OX3 0BW, England
PEOPLE'S REPUBLIC OF CHINA	Pergamon Press, Qianmen Hotel, Beijing, People's Republic of China
FEDERAL REPUBLIC OF GERMANY	Pergamon Press, Hammerweg 6, D-6242 Kronberg, Federal Republic of Germany
BRAZIL	Pergamon Editora, Rua Eça de Queiros, 346, CEP 04011, São Paulo, Brazil
AUSTRALIA	Pergamon Press (Aust.) Pty., P.O. Box 544, Potts Point, NSW 2011, Australia
JAPAN	Pergamon Press, 8th Floor, Matsuoka Central Building, 1-7-1 Nishishinjuku, Shinjuku-ku, Tokyo 160, Japan
CANADA	Pergamon Press Canada, Suite 104, 150 Consumers Road, Willowdale, Ontario M2J 1P9, Canada

First printing 1987

Library of Congress Cataloging in Publication Data

Agras, W. Stewart.
   Eating disorders.

   (Psychology practitioner guidebooks)
   Bibliography: p.
   1. Appetite disorders--Treatment. 2. Bulimia--
Treatment. 3. Obesity--Treatment. 4. Anorexia nervosa--
Treatment. I. Title. [DNLM: 1. Anorexia Nervosa--
therapy. 2. Appetite Disorders--therapy. 3. Obesity--
therapy. WM 175 A277e]
RC552.A72A37 1987   616.85'2   86-22593
ISBN 0-08-033646-9
ISBN 0-08-033645-0 (soft)

Printed in Great Britain by A. Wheaton & Co. Ltd., Exeter

Contents

Acknowledgements

This book is based in part upon the day-to-day work of the Stanford Eating Disorders Clinic staff who, over the years of my association with them, have been responsible for making many innovative suggestions regarding the assessment and treatment of their patients. In particular, I would like to mention Dr. John Schneider, Associate Director of the clinic, Dr. Susan Raeburn, and Dr. Bruce Arnow, who have been my colleagues for many years. The nursing and medical staff of the Stanford Comprehensive Medicine Unit, where many severely affected patients with eating disorders are treated, have also by their devotion to the care of patients provided an exemplary model of treatment for this book. In this regard I would particularly like to mention Dr. Lorrin Koran, the Medical Director of that unit, for his support and input into the treatment program.

No book of this scope would be possible without the vigorous interchange of ideas between research workers in the field; thanks, therefore, are due to my many colleagues from a number of countries, whose work and ideas are referenced in the text. Finally, this book and some of the research from our laboratory reported in it, has been partly supported by Grants # MH 38637 from the National Institute of Mental Health and # AM 37150 from the National Institute of Arthritis, Diabetes, and Digestive and Kidney Diseases.

Chapter 1
The Eating Disorders: Scope of the Problem

As we shall see, the incidence of the eating disorders — obesity, bulimia, and anorexia nervosa — is increasing. Because of this, more and more therapists are being faced with the difficult task of treating one or another of these related problems. The aim of this book is to describe in a practical manner the latest approaches to the treatment of the eating disorders in the adolescent or adult.

The principles underlying the treatment of obesity have been well formulated for many years, albeit with continual refinement of the less than satisfactory therapeutic methods in a large number of controlled studies. The treatment of bulimia, because of the relative rarity of this problem in our clinics until recently, has not been as well worked out. Newly published research has, however, helped to delineate the main principles of treatment for this newcomer to the eating disorders scene. Although anorexia nervosa has been of concern to therapists for many years, treatment research has been limited by the relative rarity of the disorder (Agras & Kraemer, 1983). Nonetheless, the essential treatment approaches have been well established in specialized centers. Thus we are in a position to describe the treatment strategies for each of the three disorders of eating in some detail.

Following a general introduction in this chapter delineating some of the issues underlying treatment, separate chapters are devoted to the assessment of the eating disorders; the treatment of obesity; to extensions of the basic program, including new developments in computer therapy for obesity; the treatment of bulimia; and the treatment of anorexia nervosa. In each chapter the principles and practice of treatment are described, and references are given to sources, such as treatment manuals, for therapist or patient.

The problem of managing caloric balance lies at the core of the three eating disorders. Obesity is undoubtedly the most common form of malnourishment in Western society, and is a condition of multifactorial etiology. Although bio-

1

logic factors influence the individual's ability to maintain a satisfactory caloric balance, the influence of environment is also clear. Looking at obesity from the larger historical perspective highlights the influence of environmental factors upon caloric balance. In societies in which there are not sufficient calories to provide an adequate diet, such as in times of famine, everyone will be thin and many will die prematurely. As the amount of food at the disposal of a society increases, food, still being a relatively scarce commodity, will become the pursuit of the wealthy and thus the upper social strata will be fat. Europe in the middle ages provides an example of this distribution of fatness. Curiously, though, as the amount of food further increases to become a common and hence less desirable commodity, the wealthy become thinner and those in the lower social classes become increasingly overweight. The pursuit of thinness by social-opinion leaders may account in part for the recent emergence of bulimia as a widespread problem, and for the increasing prevalance of anorexia nervosa.

DEFINITIONS

Obesity may be defined as an excessive accumulation of body fat, that is, an amount of fat that impairs health. This amount differs by gender, for it is clear that women need more body fat, on the average, to maintain health than do men. *Adiposity* should be used to denote the total amount of an individual's body fat. The term *overweight* refers to a more arbitrary classification of individuals with reference to population norms, often adjusted for sex, height, and age. According to the National Institutes of Health Consensus Conference on Obesity (1985), weight reduction should be recommended for individuals with a body weight in excess of 20% of desirable weight. Fatness, on the other hand, not only reflects adiposity but also refers to body shape in reference to societal standards in a particular culture at a particular time.

Although obesity is easy to define, it is not simple to measure, because the amount of excess fat needed to maintain health is neither easy to define nor easy to assess. The most common and accurate methods of measuring total body fat (not the amount needed to maintain health), such as underwater weighing, are not easily available, nor are they acceptable to many individuals. Measures of skinfold thickness, although providing a useful indication of adiposity at various body sites, are not technically easy to obtain; thus the error of measurement is relatively large. Luckily, Body Mass Index (BMI) (weight/height^2), an easily obtained, relatively error-free measure, correlates well with more complex measures of adiposity such as underwater weighing and skinfold thickness, thus providing a useful clinical indicator of adiposity and degree of overweight.

Both anorexia nervosa and bulimia represent a fear of the consequences of overeating. The terms *anorexia nervosa* and *bulimia* are listed as mental disorders in the *Diagnostic and Statistical Manual of Mental Disorders, 3rd edition* (DSM-III) of the American Psychiatric Association (1980), and are defined in some detail. Neither term was defined in previous editions of the diagnostic manual. Anorexia nervosa is characterized by weight loss (and a deficit in the amount of fat needed to maintain health) in the absence of any other disease process that might explain loss in body weight. The cardinal features of anorexia nervosa included in the DSM-III manual are:

1. An intense fear of becoming obese, which does not diminish as weight loss progresses.
2. Disturbance of body image, for example, claiming to "feel fat" even when emaciated.
3. Weight loss of at least 25% of original body weight or, if under 18 years of age, weight loss from original body weight plus projected weight gain expected from growth charts may be combined to make the 25%.
4. For women, amenorrhea.

Anorexia nervosa most commonly begins in adolescence, although it may begin in childhood as early as 10 years of age, or in adult life into the thirties. Anorexia nervosa may consist of a single episode with complete remission, or it may become a chronic life-threatening condition. Although vocational functioning is often reasonably well-maintained even in the chronic anorexic, interpersonal relationships and social development are usually impaired.

Bulimia is characterized by binge eating that is experienced as being out of control, an eating pattern that is secondary to dietary restriction. The cardinal *DSM-III* criteria for the diagnosis of bulimia are:

1. Recurrent episodes of binge eating (rapid consumption of a large amount of food in a discrete period of time).
2. At least three of the following:
   (a) consumption of high-caloric, easily ingested food during a binge.
   (b) inconspicuous eating during a binge.
   (c) termination of such eating episodes by abdominal pain, sleep, social interruption, or self-induced vomiting.
   (d) repeated attempts to lose weight by severely restricted diets, self-induced vomiting, or the use of cathartics or diuretics.
   (e) frequent weight fluctuations due to alternating binges and fasts.
3. Awareness that the eating pattern is abnormal and fear of not being able to stop eating voluntarily.
4. Depressed mood and self-deprecating thoughts following eating binges.

From a clinical viewpoint, it is the presence of frequent binge eating and purging, usually exceeding one episode per week and often occurring at least daily, that characterizes the bulimic patient. The proposed revision of *DSM-III* recognizes this by adding a criterion for a "minimum average of two binge-eating episodes per week for at least 3 months." Bulimia usually begins in adolescence, and appears to be a socially transmitted disease, in that purging techniques are often learned from friends or from the media. The bulimic is often more motivated to seek help than is the anorexic, and interpersonal and sexual functioning is less disturbed in the bulimic than in the anorexic patient. Impulsive behaviors such as stealing (for example, stealing food to maintain the expensive habit of binge eating) and drug use or alcoholism are frequently seen in bulimic individuals.

Fairburn and Garner (1986) have recently argued that the central feature of bulimia is the concern about body image, and that the *DSM-III* diagnostic criteria do not take this central issue into account. This suggestion would separate binge eating with or without purging and without a body-image concern (a state of affairs often found in the obese) from bulimia. These investigators also suggest that the full syndrome be named bulimia nervosa, thus distinguishing symptom from syndrome. They also suggest that degree of weight loss should not be a diagnostic feature, thus bulimia nervosa would be applied also to the "anorexic" patient who demonstrates binge eating and purging. This would narrow the current definition of anorexia nervosa to those who manage their concerns about body image by starvation and excessive activity alone.

This would separate out four distinct adult eating disorders in addition to obesity: binge eating (characterized solely by binge eating), bulimia (characterized by binge eating and purging not accompanied by a body image disturbance), bulimia nervosa, and anorexia nervosa.

EPIDEMIOLOGY OF THE
EATING DISORDERS

Anorexia Nervosa

That the frequency of at least one eating disorder, anorexia nervosa, is increasing is demonstrated in a convincing epidemiologic study from Switzerland, where the total incidence of cases under treatment was assessed for the same area at different points in time spanning 20 years (Willi & Grossman, 1983). From 1956 to 1958 the incidence of anorexia nervosa for females between the ages of 12 and 25 years, the population at risk, was 3.98 per 100,000. This had risen to 16.76 per 100,000 during the 1973–1975 period, a fourfold increase. In populations at very high risk, for example, females of upper socioeconomic classes, the incidence may be much higher. Thus, one study showed that one severe case of anorexia nervosa was to be expected for every 250 girls enrolled in private schools in London (Crisp, Palmer, & Kalucy, 1976). In such populations anorexia nervosa is by no means a rare disorder.

Obesity

At the other end of the spectrum, overweight problems are common. Even using a conservative definition, it is estimated that one in every five Americans is overweight. The average weight for women, controlling for height, has increased by 5 to 6 pounds over the last 20 years (Bureau of the Census, 1983) suggesting that the prevalence of obesity is increasing. About 15% of men and 20% of women are more than 20% above desirable weight. Such individuals have a reduced life expectancy of 2 years at age 30, 1.6 years at age 45, and 1.2 years at age 60, according to data from the Metropolitan Life Insurance Company (1983). The relationship between relative weight and mortality is somewhat U-shaped because underweight individuals appear to have an increased mortality ratio. As weight increases beyond average, the mortality ratios rise, although as we shall see later, the excess mortality from overweight appears to be confined to those in the upper decile of relative weight. There is also a clear relationship between obesity and cardiovascular risk factors such as hypertension, hypercholesterolemia, and diabetes.

It has recently been suggested that the distribution of body fat may be an important predictor of morbidity and mortality. Adipocyte metabolism varies between fat sites, with abdominal and flank fat deposits being the most active, that is, easily stored and easily mobilized, and thigh deposits being less active. Abdominal fat appears to be more closely associated with the various metabolic problems of obesity than is peripherally distributed fat. Women tend to have fat deposited in buttocks and thighs, whereas men tend toward an abdominal distribution of fat, differences that are apparent in infancy (Smith, 1985). A simple measure of fat distribution is the ratio of waist to hip circumferences.

Bulimia

Unlike obesity and anorexia nervosa, data on the epidemiology of bulimia were not obtained until relatively recently. It is the view of most clinicians that bulimia was a relatively rare disorder before 1980. In the Stanford Eating Disorders Clinic, for example, the annual number of cases of bulimia did not exceed 10 before 1979. Beginning in 1980, however, the case load dramatically increased, so that now some 200 cases are seen each year. To properly estimate the prevalence of bulimia, a randomly selected sample of the general population should be examined. No such study exists. All the surveys are drawn from particular groups of individuals unlikely to be representative of the general population, for example college students. Stangler and Printz (1980) reported a 3.8% prevalence of bulimia in 500 college students whose mean age was 25 years. Because women were affected far more frequently than men, the prevalence of diagnosed bulimia in women was 5.9%. Other studies of similar populations report similar frequencies of the disorder. One of the best studies was recently reported by Cooper and Fairburn (1983), who examined women attending a family-planning clinic in England. Twenty-one percent of such women reported binge eating episodes, 2.9% had used vomiting to control weight at one time or another, and some 1.9% met the criteria for the diagnosis of bulimia. This figure is probably the most realistic estimate for the prevalence of bulimia in young women. Bulimia thus has become a frequent problem. Moreover, bulimia, like anorexia nervosa, may be increasing in prevalence. A sampling of a college population at a 3-year interval revealed a threefold increase in (at least weekly) binge eating and purging from 1.0% to 3.2% (Pyle, Halvorson, Neuman, & Mitchell, 1986).

Binge Eating

Binge eating is one characteristic common to the three eating disorders. Nearly 50% of the obese binge, with about one quarter meeting *DSM-III* criteria for bulimia—for which self-induced vomiting is not required. In anorexia nervosa the rate of binge eating (and self-induced vomiting) exceeds 50% of the population. Binge eating appears to result from excessive dietary restriction, particularly skipping meals such as breakfast and lunch, which leads to excessive hunger by mid-afternoon, thus increasing the probability of binge eating. Dieting, in turn, seems to be a response to self-perceived fatness. Thus body-image dissatisfaction, a low ideal weight, and food deprivation or restricted eating are key cognitive and behavioral aspects of binge eating, bulimia, anorexia nervosa, and some cases of obesity. It is tempting to view the spectrum of the eating disorders as depending upon the degree of dissatisfaction with body image and of restricted eating. The obese nonbinger would be low on such a scale, the obese binger higher, the bulimic higher again, and the anorexic at the extreme end of the scale. Therapy for anorexia nervosa, bulimia, and the obese binge eater must then address the behaviors and cognitions associated with distorted body image, excessive dietary restriction and its periodic breakdown, and the struggle against hunger and binge eating. Therapy for the eating disorders must also address the environmental factors predisposing towards overeating, including better control of foods in the personal environment.

ETIOLOGY OF THE
EATING DISORDERS

Social Factors in Obesity

In the Midtown Manhattan Survey, the prevalence of obesity in the lowest social class was some 5 times that of the highest social class (Stunkard, D'Aquili, Fox, & Filion, 1972). This relatively low prevalence of obesity amongst the wealthy, who tend to be opinion leaders, has led to changes in the standards for a fashionable figure for women. A full figure that is the height of fashion at one time is abjured at another. These changes, in turn, may influence the incidence of the eating disorders, particularly bulimia and anorexia nervosa, which, as we have seen, is increasing over time. In recent years, a pattern of young women being dissatisfied with their body shape has been repeatedly documented. In one study (Dwyer, Feldman, Seltzer, & Mayer, 1969), in which high-school students were interviewed, the investigators found that 80% of women seniors, but less than 20% of male seniors wished to lose weight. Some 30% of the females but only 6% of males reported being on a diet. In a study from Sweden, Nylander (1971) reported that the number of girls who "felt fat" increased with age, with 50% of the 14-year-old group and 70% of the 18-year-old girls reporting dissatisfaction with their bodies.

This shifting trend in the socially desirable shape for women is documented in a study of three women's magazines from 1900 to the present day (Agras and Kirkley, 1986). An index of thinness was devised and was calculated for randomly selected pictures of women from each of these magazines. As can be seen in Figure 1.1, the "ideal" look for women has indeed changed over the years, from plump in the first decade of the century, to the thin long look of the 1920s, to a full figure once more in the 1940s and 1950s, and then once again to a thinner body shape. Yet in the 1920s, when extreme body thinness was depicted in advertisements, there was no trend toward bulimia as far as can be discerned from an examination of the medical literature of the time. This may be

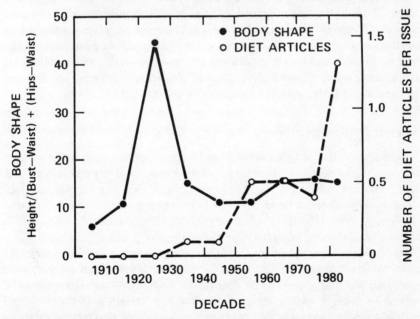

FIGURE 1.1. The Body Shape of Women as Depicted in Pictures and Advertisements in Three Women's Magazines from 1900 to the Present Day (the Higher the Point on This Scale, the Thinner the Body Shape), Together with the Prevalence of Diet Articles in the Same Magazines. (From "Bulimia: Theories of Etiology" by W. S. Agras and B. G. Kirkley, in *Handbook of Eating Disorders: Physiology, Psychology, and Treatment of Obesity, Anorexia, and Bulimia* (p. 370), edited by K. D. Brownell and J. P. Foreyt, 1986, New York: Basic Books. Copyright 1986 by Basic Books. Reprinted by permission.)

explained by the frequency of diet articles in the same periodicals. As shown in Figure 1.1, the number of diet articles was extremely low in the 1920s, began to increase in the 1940s, and then leveled off until the 1970s when a very sharp increase occurred. It would seem that in the 1920s women changed their body shape by altering their dress styles, whereas in the 1970s and 1980s women achieved these changes by dieting.

Similar trends were reported in a study of the contestants for the Miss America Pageant (Garner, Garfinkel, Schwartz, & Thompson, 1980). The contestants' weights, controlled for height, have decreased significantly since 1960. In contrast, as noted earlier, the average weight for women, again controlled for changes in height, has increased by 5 or 6 pounds over the last 20 years (Bureau of the Census, 1983). Thus women today are caught in a not very desirable situation. On the one hand, there has been an increase in average body weight, probably associated with the increased availability of food and a decrease in activity levels. On the other hand, the ideal body shape for women has become thinner. It is from this conflict, between biological reality and social standards, that the recent increase in the prevalence of both bulimia and anorexia nervosa arises. The bulimic is maintaining a thin figure while consuming a large amount of food, a "sensible" solution to the conflict. The anorexic solves the conflict by exerting extreme control of food intake often accompanied by excessive energy expenditure. For the obese in a culture of plenty, excessive deposition of body fat may reflect a normal physiological response. Returning to "normal weight" may, for these individuals, represent a state of chronic starvation.

Biologic Factors in Obesity

In addition to the influence of social and environmental factors in the etiology of the eating disorders, the therapist must take into account what is known about biologic factors influencing food intake and caloric management, for such factors may limit what can be accomplished in treatment. Obesity tends to run in families. A recent large-scale adoptive study confirmed that adiposity tends to follow that of natural parents rather than adoptive parents (Stunkard et al., 1986). Although the mechanism through which obesity is expressed genetically is not known, it seems likely that three factors are involved: high adipose tissue lipophilia, probably caused by an abnormally high lipoprotein lipase response to food ingestion; a low metabolic response to food intake, with the obese not burning as many calories as the nonobese; and an exaggerated predisposition to develop fat cells.

Evidence suggests that once acquired, fat cells do not decrease in number, although the size of fat cells may vary. Early in life, children who will become obese have a greater number of fat cells than nonobese children, and a more rapid increase in the number and size of such cells during childhood and early adolescence. Studies have also shown that when the overweight person is put on a low-calorie diet, oxygen consumption, a measure of energy utilization, is reduced to compensate for the caloric deficit. This compensation may occur quite rapidly, so that the benefits of lowered caloric intake may be largely offset in a period of a few weeks. This mechanism may underlie the problem noted by many overweight persons attempting to diet, namely losing weight for a few weeks and then reaching a plateau. Discouragement may then lead to quitting the weight-loss program and the regaining of weight.

Exercise may offset this compensatory mechanism to some extent, increasing metabolic rate at least temporarily. A regular program of increased activity thus forms a central component of most weight-loss programs, bringing with it three benefits: direct usage of calories through body movement, increase in metabolic rate that enhances the use of calories, and enhanced muscular, pulmonary, and cardiovascular function. Activity levels may also influence the development of adiposity. There is little evidence that activity influences obesity during the first 2 years of life. In a fairly large study using an ambulatory monitor to assess activity levels at 18 months of age in our laboratory, no relationship between activity and adiposity, either concurrently or prospectively, was found. On the other hand, activity levels were found to be negatively correlated with adiposity in a study of 5- to 7-year-old children using the same measurement system (Berkowitz, Agras, Korner, Kraemer, & Zeanah, 1985). This suggests that lack of activity becomes an increasingly important contributor to obesity during the course of childhood.

The National Children and Youth Fitness Survey recently studied a national probability sample of more than 10,000 5th- through 12th-grade students. Physical fitness was assessed in part by cardiorespiratory endurance (the 1 mile run/walk test). Preliminary data from this large study found that skinfold measures decreased steadily as fitness increased, suggesting that the more active children were less adipose (Blair, Clark, & Kohl, 1986). Higher activity levels are also associated with a decrease in mortality rates. In a follow-up study of nearly 20,000 Harvard alumni, death rates were one-quarter to one-third lower among alumni expending 2,000 or more kcal each week in exercise, than among less active men (Paffenberger, Hyde, Wing, & Hsieh, 1986). Much of the excess mortality among less active participants in this study was due to cardiovascular and respiratory disease.

The development of adiposity from infancy to adolescence, as reflected by BMI, is shown in Figure 1.2. Adiposity increases dramatically during the first year of life and then declines, to rise once more in early childhood. As also shown, those who will become obese in adolescence (and hence have a 28:1 chance of being an obese adult) tend to be more adipose at birth, to reach peak adiposity later during infancy, to show less decline in adiposity by 2 years of age, and to show an earlier rise in BMI during childhood, than those who will remain normal weight. This developmental pattern closely approximates that for fat-cell number. From a developmental viewpoint there are three critical stages: the rate of increase in adiposity during the first year of life, the degree of loss of adipose tissue in the second year of life, and the timing of the increase in adiposity during childhood.

A few factors influencing the development of adiposity during childhood have now been identified. First, infants with a higher BMI at birth tend to be more adipose at 1 or 2 years of age, although this association tends to disappear by about 8 years of age. Most studies, but not all, suggest that bottle feeding, perhaps combined with the early introduction of solid food, leads to an increase in adiposity during the first and second years of life, as compared with children who are breast-fed, but no differences were found between bottle-fed and breast-fed children who were followed prospectively to the age of 8 years (Dine et al., 1979; Fomon, Rogers, Ziegler, Nelson, & Thomas, 1984; Kramer et al., 1985). Caloric intake during infancy also influences later adiposity. In work from our own laboratory, infants who consumed more calories during laboratory feedings were more adipose at 2 years of age.

An obese "eating style" has also been detected during the second year of life. Laboratory studies have shown that children who will be more obese at 2 years of age tend to eat a similar number of calories more quickly than those who will

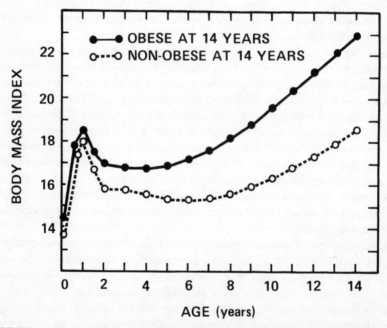

FIGURE 1.2. The Body Mass Index (BMI) of a Cohort of Children Followed from Birth to 14 Years of Age, with Frequent Measurement of Body Height and Weight. BMI (Reflecting the Amount of Body Fat) for Those Who Were Obese at 14 Years of Age Versus Those Who Were of Normal Weight is Shown.

be of normal weight. Similar obese eating styles, characterized by rapid eating, less chewing of food, and more drinking during meals, have been detected during childhood and adult life in a number of studies (Adams, Ferguson, Stunkard, & Agras, 1978; Drabman, Cordua, Hammer, Jarvie, & Horton, 1979), although other studies do not find any relationship between eating style and adiposity (Stunkard & Kaplan, 1977). Whether rectifying this eating behavior leads to a reduction in weight is not clear; however, many weight-loss programs incorporate procedures to modify these eating behaviors. Despite these encouraging findings, it is important to note that only 25% of the variance for adiposity at 2 years of age can be explained by known factors.

Factors Affecting Anorexia Nervosa and Bulimia

Even less is known about the factors influencing the development of anorexia nervosa and bulimia, although a large proportion of these individuals report a mild degree of overweight before the onset of the disorder. Crisp (1983) hypothesizes that a "weight phobia" is central to anorexia nervosa, and that anorexics avoid many of the social consequences of adolescence by reducing their weight, obliterating secondary sexual characteristics, and returning to a prepubertal role. In a study of 34 twins and 1 set of triplets, the concordance for anorexia nervosa was 55% for identical pairs, and 7% for the dizygotic pairs. This strongly suggests, as is the case for obesity, that genetic factors play an important role in the etiology of anorexia nervosa (Crisp, Hall, & Holland, 1985). The mechanism by which genetic influences produce the syndrome of anorexia nervosa is quite unknown. Despite many careful studies, no primary biochemical abnormalities have been found in the anorexic. All the metabolic changes so far described are secondary to the weight loss. Some studies have suggested that there is an excess of major depression in the first-degree relatives of anorexic and bulimic persons (Hudson, Laffer, & Pope, 1982). This has led to the use of antidepressant medication in the treatment of both anorexia nervosa and bulimia.

According to a survey of nearly 500 bulimic women conducted by Cooper and Fairburn (1983) the mean age of onset of binge eating was 18.4 years, an age corresponding to the highest rates of bodily dissatisfaction among women. Nearly 50% of these women were more than 15% above the mean population weight, and over a quarter were 20% above the population mean. The most likely sequence of events is that the pre-bulimic woman restricts food intake because of body dissatisfaction, and that this restriction leads to binge eating. In order to control the weight gain associated with this behavior, many of these individuals resort to purging, which begins, on the average, about 1 year after the onset of binge eating.

Laboratory studies comparing normal and restrained eaters (i.e., individuals actively dieting) given increasing caloric pre-loads and then asked to rate three flavors of ice cream, revealed that normals ate progressively less ice cream as the pre-load increased, and that restrained eaters consumed progressively more (Herman & Mack, 1975). Once a food rule is broken (a high pre-load), binge eating tends to occur. Later studies demonstrated that the perception of consuming a high-calorie pre-load was almost as powerful as an actual high-calorie pre-load in setting off overconsumption of ice cream.

These findings suggest that cognitive distortions concerning food consumption must be dealt with in therapy for bulimia. The same group of investigators also demonstrated that restrained eaters ate more when made anxious before a test meal, whereas unrestrained eaters ate less. This finding suggests that the bulimic, while in an anxious or depressed state, will be more likely to binge. On the other hand, the binge-purge cycle, with its accompanying undernutrition, may in turn lead to anxiety and depression that then aggravates the problem behaviors of binge eating and purging. The implications for therapy differ between these hypotheses. In the first case, anxiety and depression should be attended to as a separate issue in the bulimic, because it aggravates the problem. In the second case, anxiety and depression would be expected to clear up once nutritional balance was reinstated. In both cases, it is clear that therapy must be directed toward reversing the restricted eating pattern (which often consists of skipping meals such as breakfast and lunch and eating a very restricted range of foods) and reinstating a normal frequency of meals and a more normal dietary content.

Biologic factors also play a part in increasing appetite for sweet foods: many bulimics complain about a "carbohydrate" craving. Animal studies reveal that when the animals were deprived of food in short-term experiments, sweet-tasting foods that are normally avoided became preferred. Animals at an abnormally low body weight show similar preferences. A craving for simple carbohydrates thus is found in both acute and chronic food-deprivation states (Cabanac & Duclaux, 1970; Mook & Cseh, 1981). Overweight individuals who completed a weight-reduction program also reported an increased preference for, and consumption of, sweet foods (Rodin, Slochower, & Fleming, 1977). Individuals who chronically restrain their food consumption, such as bulimics, may paradoxically increase their desire for, and consumption of, sweet foods.

HEALTH PROBLEMS ASSOCIATED WITH THE EATING DISORDERS

Both relative overweight and underweight are accompanied by an increased risk to health and to life. All the eating disorders are associated with increased illness because both anorexics, and to a lesser extent bulimics, are underweight. Obesity is accompanied by physiologic changes such as increased blood pressure and low density lipoprotein (LDL) cholesterol, and a decreased glucose tolerance.

Obesity

Among the high-risk diseases with which the obese are afflicted at a higher rate than the nonobese are essential hypertension, diabetes mellitus, heart disease, and gall bladder disease. In addition, the obese have a greater risk of developing lethal complications following surgery. Respiratory insufficiency and sleep apnea also occur in the obese. A recent study underlines the fact that complications of obesity may begin in childhood (Freedman et al., 1985). In a cohort of children followed from 5 years to 12 years of age it was found that LDL cholesterol levels were correlated with change in indices of adiposity such as skin-fold thickness, with the more adipose children having higher levels of LDL cholesterol.

Less life-threatening complications also occur in obesity. These include hernias due to stretching and thinning of the abdominal musculature, osteoarthritis due to increased wear and tear on joints, and menstrual disturbances. Impaired agility may lead to increased accident-proneness. In addition, largely due to the negative reaction of others towards the obese, there are psychological complications, which include an increased prevalence of anxiety and depression. This predisposition to a variety of ailments forms the main rationale for the treatment of obesity.

Weight loss exerts a beneficial effect on essential hypertension, hypercholesterolemia, adult-onset diabetes mellitus, and sleep apnea. In the best study to date, over 100 obese hypertensives, both on and off medication, were allocated to weight-loss therapy or a control group (Reisin et al., 1978). To control for the effects of salt reduction, which automatically accompanies decreased caloric intake, the subjects were prescribed a high-salt diet, and sodium excretion was monitored. Blood pressures were significantly lower in those who lost weight, whether or not they were on medication. In a related study, not only was blood pressure found to fall significantly more in young overweight hypertensive patients who lost weight, but left ventricular mass was also significantly reduced (MacMahon, Wilcken, & Macdonald, 1986). The authors concluded that weight reduction may prevent left ventricular hypertrophy, a serious complication of elevated blood pressure.

Weight loss also exerts a beneficial effect on cholesterol levels, although the short-term effect may be more marked in men than in women (Brownell & Stunkard, 1981). In men who lost weight, HDL cholesterol was raised and LDL cholesterol was lowered, both of these changes being in a beneficial direction. In women, however, both HDL and LDL cholesterol levels were lowered, the overall result being of little protective value against coronary heart disease. In a longer study, however, women whose cholesterol levels had behaved in a similar manner to those in the study just described showed a drop in LDL cholesterol levels and a rise in HDL cholesterol at 6-month follow-up, changes that were significantly correlated with changes in BMI (Follick, Abrams, Smith, Henderson, & Herbert, 1984).

A controlled study of weight loss in persons with sleep apnea also demon-strated marked benefit for those in a weight-loss group versus those who were in the control condition (Smith, Gold, Meyers, Haponik, & Bleecker, 1985). Those who lost weight showed a marked reduction in the frequency of sleep apnea as well as an increased oxygenation during the remaining apneic events. The con-tribution of a behavioral weight-loss program to the treatment of adult-onset diabetes has also been investigated (Wing, Epstein, Nowalk, Scott, Koeske, & Hagg, in press). At 1-year follow-up the groups had lost between 4.1 and 8.2 kg, and some 70% of the participants were able to reduce their insulin or oral hypoglycemic medication.

Although there are clear benefits from weight reduction, there are also costs. These include the monetary cost of therapy, hazards secondary to poorly super-vised or poorly conceived therapy, and the hazards of over-rapid weight loss, including loss of lean body mass and adverse biochemical changes. Experiences of repeated failure to maintain weight losses may also cause discouragement or depression. These factors must be taken into account when counseling individ-uals regarding weight loss. In addition, for adolescent females, the risk of pro-voking bulimia or even anorexia nervosa during the course of a weight-loss program should be kept in mind.

Bulimia

The bulimic is also faced with risks to health. These include menstrual prob-lems associated with weight loss; dental cavities due to eating simple sugars and enamel loss from repeated vomiting; hypokalemia (low potassium levels) due to the electrolyte loss associated with repeated vomiting or the use of pur-gatives, in combination with deficient intake—which in turn predisposes towards cardiac arrythmias and renal damage. Other complications associ-ated with repeated vomiting include swelling of the parotid glands, chronic hoarseness, and esophageal tearing with bleeding. More rarely, binge eating will lead to rupture of the stomach. Psychological sequelae of binge eating and purging include dysphoria or depression, excessive preoccupation with food and body image or weight to the exclusion of more usual concerns, and occasionally, disturbances of intellectual functioning due to poor nutrition, dehydration, and electrolyte disturbances. It is quite remarkable, however, that the largest number of bulimics are in relatively good health. A recent study in which detailed medical evaluations were carried out on 39 bulimics found little evidence of serious medical disorder. Low body weight was corre-lated with hypokalemia, although only 10% of subjects had abnormally low levels of serum potassium. In addition, elevated serum amylase levels due to salivary overactivity were found in 62% of patients (Jacobs & Schneider, 1985).

Anorexia Nervosa

In addition to the complications associated with bulimia, the anorexic, because of extreme weight loss, suffers from cessation of menstruation, cold intolerance, dry skin often covered by fine body hair, cold and blue extremities, peripheral edema, bradycardia, and hypotension (low blood pressure). Depression more extreme than that usually associated with bulimia often occurs, and it should be remembered that about half the fatalities due to anorexia nervosa are caused by suicide. Any intercurrent illness, such as pneumonia, carries more risk than it does for the individual who is at normal weight.

Summary

Overall, the highest health risks occur in those individuals who are at the extremes of body weight, namely the severely obese and the anorexic. However, any consistent deviation from normal weight (controlled for age and height) predisposes towards health problems. The major rationale for treating individuals with eating disorders stems from the actual or potential deleterious consequences for the health of the individual associated with each disorder and the psychological suffering accompanying these common problems. The treatment of the eating disorders should occur within the broader context of health improvement and disease prevention, rather than concentrating solely upon the cosmetic consequences of changes in weight. This rationale for behavior change should begin to emerge during initial assessment as the therapist and patient review the pros and cons of treatment.

Chapter 2
The Eating Disorders:
Assessment

The assessment of any one of the eating disorders is similar to the others because issues of body shape, weight control, eating behavior, nutrition, and health are common to them all. The focus of assessment will shift, however, depending upon the condition being addressed, the age of the patient, and the motivation for treatment. Generally speaking, the motivation of the obese patient concerning treatment and the associated behavior changes is excellent, whereas that of the anorexic is poor. For the bulimic, as is often the case, motivation lies somewhere between that of the other two conditions. Although the social environment is important in all three eating disorders, the degree of involvement of the family will necessarily differ between the middle-aged obese client, the young adult bulimic, and the adolescent anorexic. In the latter case, involvement of the family in the process of assessment is imperative; in the other cases it will be left to the judgment of the therapist.

Assessment consists of three phases:

1. Completion of a screening questionnaire that allows much of the basic information concerning the problem to be easily obtained in a systematic fashion.
2. This is followed by (usually) one interview to clarify the basic history of the problem and to make an accurate diagnosis of the main disorder and any associated psychological problems.
3. Self-monitoring of the problem behavior for several days forms the last element in a detailed assessment, in turn setting the stage for therapeutic recommendations, and for treatment.

A SCREENING QUESTIONNAIRE
FOR THE EATING DISORDERS

An eating disorders screening questionnaire, which can be filled out by the patient before the initial interview, is reproduced in Appendix A. This questionnaire has been in use at the Stanford Eating Disorders Clinic for many years and has proven useful for both clinical and research use. The questionnaire covers several areas systematically, and is designed to mesh with the format of an initial interview.

The first items ask for identifying information from the client and information about present occupation, schooling, and living situation. The questionnaire then addresses weight, asking for present weight, ideal weight, and satisfaction with body image, as well as the attitudes of family and friends towards the client's weight. A chart is appended, allowing for a detailed lifetime history of weight changes, including the patient's assessment of how over- or underweight they were at various periods in their life, as well as the ways in which they attempted to alter their weight. This section is followed by detailed questions pertaining to binge eating and purging, followed by an assessment of activity levels. Finally, a medical history and brief family history are requested.

In addition to this questionnaire, it is useful to assess the extent of the patient's depression using the Beck Depression Inventory (Beck, Ward, Mendelsohn, Mock, & Erbaugh, 1961) because many patients with eating disorders have associated depression or dysphoria. Other screening instruments more useful in research than in clinical practice are the Eating Attitudes Scale (Garner & Garfinkel, 1979) and an assertiveness inventory (Gambrill & Richey, 1975). With this information available, the therapist is in a position to conduct an initial interview with the patient. Because evaluation of each eating disorder has its own specific focus and problems, the assessment process for each will be considered separately. In each case the first step in the interview process is to clarify any missing or obscure items on the questionnaire.

OBESITY

In the case of obesity several clinical issues likely to affect the course of treatment should be addressed in the initial interview. These include:

1. The degree of the patient's obesity.
2. The presence or absence of binge eating.
3. The extent of the patient's depression.
4. The presence of current life problems that might interfere with treatment.
5. The patient's motivation for treatment.
6. The presence or absence of concurrent health problems.

From the viewpoint of treatment, obesity may be classified quite simply into mild, moderate, and severe types. Mild obesity, which is best treated with a behavioral approach, ranges from 15% overweight to an upper limit of perhaps 35%. Moderate obesity, which presents a problem to the behavioral approach because of the extent of weight loss needed, ranges from 35 to 100% overweight. In such cases individual rather than group therapy may be indicated, and long-term treatment is essential. As we will see, the addition of a very-low-calorie diet might be considered in such cases. Severe obesity is defined as being more than 100% overweight. This degree of obesity may carry a severe risk to life, and a surgical approach to treatment (gastroplasty) should be considered. If, however, no behavioral treatment has been tried, then this, combined with a very-low-calorie diet, should be the first approach to treatment, to be backed up by surgery in case of failure.

The category into which an obese individual fits can be determined by referring to the Metropolitan Life Insurance Company tables shown in Tables 2.1 and 2.2. The recent NIH Consensus Conference on Obesity (1985) suggested that clinicians use BMI as an indicator of adiposity. The Metropolitan tables can be collapsed into a relatively simple BMI range, above which treatment should be considered. For women, the range at which treatment should be considered is 25–28, for men, 26–28. In both cases the therapist should use the lower end of the range for the taller patient, and the upper end of the range for the shorter patient. These ranges correspond to approximately the 75th percentile for both men and women, as shown in Table 2.3. These ranges are, however, well below those indicated by excess mortality risk in, for example, the Framingham study (Sorile, Gordon, & Kannel, 1980). The latter study suggests that excess mortality begins in the 31–35 range for females, and 30–34 for males, figures above the 90th percentile.

Table 2.1. Average Weights of Men: Graduated Weights (in indoor clothing) in Pounds

Height (in shoes)	15–16	17–19	20–24	Age Groups 25–29	30–39	40–49	50–59	60–69
Feet/Inches								
4'10	93	106	112	116	120	121	122	121
11	98	110	117	121	124	126	127	126
5'0	102	115	121	125	129	131	132	130
1	107	119	126	130	133	135	136	135
2	112	124	130	134	138	140	141	140
3	116	129	136	140	143	144	145	144
4	121	132	139	143	147	149	150	149
5	127	137	143	147	151	154	155	153
6	133	141	148	152	156	158	159	158
7	137	145	153	156	160	163	164	163
8	143	150	157	161	165	167	168	167
9	148	155	163	166	170	172	173	172
10	153	159	167	171	174	.176	177	176
11	159	164	171	175	179	181	182	181
6'0	162	168	176	181	184	186	187	186
1	168	174	182	186	190	192	193	191
2	173	179	187	191	195	197	198	196
3	178	185	193	197	201	203	204	200
4	184	190	198	202	206	208	209	207
5	189	195	203	207	211	213	214	212

Note: From Metropolitan Height and Weight Tables (p. 17) by the Metropolitan Life Insurance Company, 1983, New York: Society of Actuaries and Association of Life Insurance Medical Directors. Copyright 1983 by Society of Actuaries. Reprinted by permission.

Table 2.2. Average Weights of Women: Graduated Weights (in indoor clothing) in Pounds

Height (in shoes)	15-16	17-19	20-24	Age Groups 25-29	30-39	40-49	50-59	60-69
Feet/Inches								
4'8	93	95	99	103	107	111	115	117
9	97	99	101	106	110	114	118	120
10	101	103	105	110	113	118	121	123
11	105	108	110	112	115	121	125	127
5'0	109	111	112	114	118	123	127	130
1	112	115	116	119	121	127	131	133
2	117	119	120	121	124	129	133	136
3	121	123	124	125	128	133	137	140
4	123	126	127	128	131	136	141	143
5	128	129	130	132	134	139	144	147
6	131	132	133	134	137	143	147	150
7	135	136	137	138	141	147	152	155
8	138	140	141	142	145	150	156	158
9	142	145	146	148	150	155	159	161
10	146	148	149	150	153	158	162	163
11	149	150	155	156	159	162	166	167
6'0	152	154	157	159	164	168	171	172
1	155	157	159	163	168	172	175	176
2	158	160	162	166	172	176	179	180
3	161	163	165	170	176	180	183	184

Note: From *Metropolitan Height and Weight Tables* (p. 18) by the Metropolitan Life Insurance Company, 1983, New York: Society of Actuaries and Association of Life Insurance Medical Directors. Copyright 1983 by Society of Actuaries. Reprinted by permission.

Having determined the degree of the patient's obesity, which in turn will begin to point to a particular therapeutic approach, the next step is to examine the patient's eating pattern in more detail. For this the therapist should first review items 19-35 on the questionnaire (see Appendix A). As noted in the previous chapter, about 25% of overweight individuals report frequent binge eating, and such individuals appear to do less well in behavioral weight-loss programs than the nonbinge eater (Keefe, Wyshogrod, Weinberger, & Agras, 1984). The presence or absence of binge eating is ascertained by the answers to questions 19-27, and if the answers to these questions are negative, the therapist may wish to probe this area to make sure that the patient understood the questions. If binge eating is reported, then the frequency of such behavior should be ascertained, as well as the degree to which the patient feels out of control in regard to the binge food. The presence or absence of self-induced vomiting or other methods of purging such as laxative use (question 28) and body image dissatisfaction (questions 13, 14) should be ascertained, because in such cases the problem of obesity is complicated by bulimia nervosa.

Alcohol use is addressed in question 36, and if there is any suspicion of alcohol abuse the therapist should again use probing questions to reveal the full extent of the problem. Current activity levels, a most important deficit in most

Table 2.3. Percentiles of BMI for Adult Males and Females

Age	10	Males: Percentiles 25	50	75	90	Age	10	Females: Percentiles 25	50	75	90
24–29	20	22	24	27	30	24–29	19	20	22	25	30
30–32	21	23	25	28	31	30–32	19	20	23	26	31
33–44	22	23	26	28	31	33–35	19	21	23	26	31
45–50	21	24	26	28	31	36–38	20	21	23	27	31
						39–41	20	21	24	27	32
						42–50	20	22	24	28	33

obese individuals, are assessed in questions 37 and 38. In addition to the frequency and duration of physical activity, which the therapist will want to check, an estimate of the intensity of the exercise should be obtained. The final questions concern the patient's medical history and family history of obesity. A strong genetic predisposition toward obesity, combined with moderate or severe obesity, may suggest that the patient will have problems in losing weight.

During the course of the interview the therapist should have been making observations concerning objective signs of depression evident in facial expression, content of speech, and perhaps retardation of thought and speech. In addition, the Beck Depression Inventory should be scored. Usually scores above 20 will indicate a depression of some severity, although some questions are sensitive to the presence of overweightness and feelings about appearance, and thus may inflate the score. Symptoms of a current major depression, which is a contraindication to weight-loss treatment, are a depressed mood; sleep disturbance, particularly early morning awakening; appetite loss associated with weight loss; loss of energy; difficulty in concentrating; and suicidal thoughts. Less severe levels of depression do not usually interfere with weight-loss treatment.

In addition to the signs and symptoms of depression, the therapist should make some estimation of the stability of the patient's current life. An unstable life situation, such as an ongoing stressful separation or divorce, or an extremely demanding and stressful job requiring long working hours, often result in less than optimal attendance at therapy sessions, and poor compliance with therapeutic instructions. Life-styles that revolve around the consumption of food, for example, many meals eaten in restaurants with a spouse, may make weight loss very difficult, and the therapist should ascertain how easy it would be to change such behavior without threatening the personal relationships involved.

The patient's motivation for treatment should now be assessed together with the appropriateness of the patient's goals for weight loss. Although improvement in physical appearance is usually a major motivation for beginning treatment, such a motivation may be problematic because the weight loss achievable by many individuals may not alter physical appearance dramatically. To this extent the goals set by the patient may be unrealistic. The time to tackle this situation is in the initial interview. The presence of health problems may provide a more realistic motivation for weight loss. In addition, it should be remembered that small weight losses, or simply stopping the inevitable rise in weight with increasing age, can be useful in enhancing health. The benefits of a regular exercise regimen in terms of enhanced muscular strength, fitness, and cardiovascular health, should also be stressed by the therapist, as should the advantages to health of changing dietary habits. In this way, the patient can begin to set therapeutic goals that do not depend entirely upon cosmetic considerations.

The NIH Consensus Conference (1985) recommended that weight reduction should be considered in the following medical conditions:

1. Family history of, or risk factors for, adult-onset diabetes.
2. High blood pressure.
3. Hypertriglyceridemia or hypercholesterolemia.
4. Coronary disease (or atherosclerosis).
5. Gout.
6. Functional impairment due to heart disease, chronic obstructive pulmonary disease, or osteoarthritis (spine, hips, and knees, which bear weight).
7. History of childhood obesity.

If the patient is suitable for, and agreeable to, weight-loss therapy, a discussion of the program should follow naturally at this stage of assessment. This is also the time to discuss fees, including any deposit refundable upon specific behaviors, such as attending sessions. In the latter case, a written contract specifying the contingencies should be signed by both therapist and participant. The disposition of funds not returned to the patient should be clearly specified in the contract. If the therapist feels that the patient should not attempt a weight-loss regimen at this time, alternative arrangements for therapy, for example, for the treatment of alcoholism or severe depression, should be made.

If the overweight or obese patient has not had a recent physical examination, an appropriate referral should be arranged so that any associated health problems can be identified and monitored during the course of weight loss. When a very-low-calorie diet is to be prescribed it is essential that medical assessment and follow-up are built into the treatment program.

BULIMIA

The principal areas of concern associated with an initial interview in the case of bulimia are very similar to those for obesity:

1. The pattern and severity of binge eating and purging.
2. The degree of bodily dissatisfaction.
3. The degree of underweight/overweight.
4. The presence or absence of depression.
5. Complicating physical illness.
6. The patient's life situation.

The bulimic pattern is well described in the questionnaire, both in the weight history, and more particularly in questions 19–38, which cover the binge behavior and methods of purging. The caloric intake of bulimic individuals varies markedly. Some patients consume as many as 15,000 calories a day, others less than 1,000 calories. Some binges, then, may consist of eating a small amount of food that breaks the patient's "food rules." Once the food rule is broken, some patients immediately purge, whereas others go on to consume large amounts of food. Almost all bulimics demonstrate a restricted pattern of caloric intake, eating little for breakfast and for lunch, and tending to binge in the afternoons and evenings. The therapist should ask the patient to describe his or her food intake for a typical day in some detail, both for "normal" meals and for "binges." Alcohol intake, drug use and abuse, and stealing of either food or other goods, should be investigated during this phase of the interview, because these types of behavior are found from time to time among bulimics and may complicate therapy.

Once the pattern of eating has been clarified, the methods used in purging should be examined. The therapist should review the answers to questions 28, 37, and 38. To help the patient fully disclose the nature of the problem, the therapist should probe for the details of the vomiting behavior: How induced? (use of finger, automatic vomiting, use of ipecac); when and where it is induced; the use of rituals such as cleaning up afterwards; and methods used to hide the behavior. The use of diuretics, laxatives, fasting alternating with binges, and strenuous exercise should also be covered in detail, even if the patient has answered "No" to these questions.

The degree of dissatisfaction with body size and shape should be examined at this point. Questions 13 and 14 provide a beginning answer to this problem and a basis for further exploration. The precise areas of body dissatisfaction should be clarified, and the degree of rigidity of these beliefs determined by asking hypothetical questions such as "How would you feel if you were to gain 5 lb (10 lb, etc.)?" At this point some of the patient's erroneous beliefs about food, weight, and body shape can often be explicated.

Most bulimics are slightly underweight by 5 to 15%, some are of normal weight, and a few are overweight. The therapeutic approach taken may be different depending upon the patient's current weight. Should weight loss be in the 20–25% range, then restoration of normal body weight becomes the first task, with treatment of the binge eating and purging as a secondary concern. The BMI below which mortality rates are elevated above those for persons of normal weight is 18 for women and 20 for men, values that are below the 10th percentile of the population. For the overweight bulimic, attention must be directed not only toward the binge eating and purging, but also toward the accompanying obesity. Here the paradox is that by increasing the number of meals eaten during the day, total caloric intake is reduced as binge eating ceases.

The patient's physical condition should now be assessed, and patients who have not had a recent physical examination should be asked to do so before beginning therapy, so that any complicating physical disorder, such as an electrolyte imbalance, can be corrected and followed medically. As in the case of obesity, the degree of depression should be assessed. Some degree of dysphoria is a very common accompaniment of bulimia, although it is relatively rare for the diagnosis of major depression to be made. In the latter case, the option of pharmacologic treatment for the depression should be seriously considered concurrent with the treatment for the bulimia. For the most part, however, symptoms of depression improve as the patient's binge eating and purging decrease. Finally, the patient's current life situation should be explored, so that, as in the case of obesity, the extent of complicating features can be assessed before therapy is begun.

Hospitalization is infrequently indicated for the bulimic patient. The most common indication is a loss of body weight greater than 20%, and/or very frequent binge eating and purging associated with medical complications of bulimia such as hypokalemia and dehydration. Other indicators include the association of severe psychiatric disorder, such as major depression, hypomania, or schizophrenia, with the bulimia. Because the hospital is not the environment in which the behaviors associated with binge eating and purging normally occur, little progress in treating the bulimic symptoms can be expected during a hospital stay.

ANOREXIA NERVOSA

The assessment of anorexia nervosa differs from that of obesity and most cases of bulimia in that the prospective patient is often poorly motivated for treatment and is being brought for consultation by an alarmed family. The major diagnostic features of anorexia nervosa are: a weight loss greater than 25% of actual or expected body weight, a very restricted eating pattern often accompanied by excessive exercise, a fear of gaining weight combined with a distorted perception of bodily thinness, low ideal weight, and amenorrhea (in women). Use of the questionnaire together with a clinical interview will usually quickly lead to the correct diagnosis, although it should be remembered that physical illness may mimic anorexia nervosa, and that a concurrent investigation by an internist is essential for correct diagnosis.

Both the patient and family members should be interviewed during the diagnostic process, and it is usually best to see each individual separately at first, so as to gather as much independent information as possible. When a diagnosis has been reached, feedback should be given to the patient and family together so that each person involved hears the same message and has an opportunity to discuss the issues raised by the diagnosis. Such feedback should include the diagnosis, prognosis, and an outline of the treatment plan. For most cases of anorexia nervosa, inpatient treatment aimed at restoration of normal body weight will be needed. This recommendation will often raise protests from the patient, which the family must deal with. The role of the therapist is to aid the family in confronting the prospective patient on the need for hospitalization focusing upon the interpersonal processes involved. The therapist should not, however, become involved in persuading the patient to enter a hospital, because this will tend to enmesh the therapist in the family problem.

This process may take one or several sessions, depending upon the degree of resistance to treatment and the willingness of the family to confront the issues. It is often helpful to have the patient and family members visit the inpatient unit to demystify this aspect of treatment. Once the patient has indicated a willingness to enter the hospital, an initial behavioral contract (see Chapter 7, "An Inpatient Treatment Program") should be worked out, detailing the role and responsibilities of the patient, and the consequences for gaining or losing weight. This contract should be *negotiated* with the patient, thus introducing this form of interchange. The different kinds of therapy—reinforcement for weight gain, group meetings, family therapy—should be carefully explained to the entire family, and their expected role and participation in these activities made clear.

When weight loss has not reached extreme proportions (less than 15% weight loss) outpatient treatment may be indicated (see Chapter 7, "Outpatient Treatment for Anorexia Nervosa"). The same process of feedback should be used as in the case of inpatient treatment, and the potential necessity of hospitalization, if weight is not gained, should be explained to the patient and family, and acceptance of this should be made an integral aspect of treatment. Many patients will try to gain weight to avoid hospitalization, and the prior agreement for hospital care removes a potential problem from the therapist should the patient not gain weight. A treatment contract should be worked out and signed by the patient and therapist.

ASSESSMENT OF
THERAPEUTIC PROGRESS

The methods by which therapeutic progress will be monitored also form an aspect of initial assessment because baseline measures should be obtained at this time in order to make comparisons with later measures. For both obesity and anorexia nervosa, the determination of weight under standard conditions will form one of the main outcome measures. Such weights should be obtained using a balance scale resting upon a hard surface (soft surfaces may lead to inaccurate weights), calibrated to zero. Both the therapist and patient will wish to maintain a simple weight chart. In the case of obesity, waist and hip measurements may also be useful to monitor the progress of loss of body fat in these areas. Some therapists add thigh measures. It is sometimes the case that improvements in body shape will mean more to individuals than weight losses.

In the case of bulimia, weight will usually form only an ancillary outcome measure, because most bulimics are of reasonably normal weight. Only an occasional estimation of weight will be needed in most cases. For bulimia, self-monitoring of food intake, binge eating, and purging will provide the most useful data for determining progress. Patients should be encouraged to maintain a graph of purging episodes throughout treatment. Self-monitoring is also useful for obesity and anorexia nervosa, although in the latter case, resistance to treatment often makes such information impossible to obtain during the assessment phase. Measures of depression also form a useful process measure in all three eating disorders.

A typical self-monitoring form for use with obese patients, which has been filled out to illustrate the necessary detail, is shown in Figure 2.1. Each instance of food intake is recorded, along with the time of day, type of food, quantity of food, type of preparation, and length of the eating episode. In addition, eating speed estimated on a 1–7 scale from slow to fast; hunger rated in a similar manner, the place in which the eating occurred, other activities being engaged in simultaneously, and mood and thoughts are also indicated. On the same form the amount of activity is also recorded.

In the case of bulimia a slightly different form may be used, as illustrated in Figure 2.2. In addition to the time of day, food type and quantity, and circumstances of eating, several other items, more relevant for the bulimic, have been added. These include whether or not the meal was defined as a binge, the degree of fullness after the food was consumed, purging (defined as self-induced vomiting), and use of laxatives. The blank column may be used to monitor individualized aspects of behavior, for example, exercise where this is excessive.

The rationale for the use of self-monitoring should be carefully explained to the patient, pointing out that accurate data concerning the problem need to be collected so that both patient and therapist can better know which behaviors should be addressed. It should also be pointed out that patients who continue to monitor their behavior tend to progress better than patients who do not. Following this, the method of collecting data should be gone over carefully, including:

1. The need to complete the record immediately after the behavior has been engaged in, rather than at the end of the day.
2. The need for a detailed record. Here the example of Chris Coe (Figure 2.1) may be used.
3. The usefulness of the record to the patient, in terms of making meal planning easier and in terms of behavior change.

With this task completed the stage has been set for therapy to begin.

NAME Chris Coe   DAY Thursday 9/15/82

	Eating										Activity		
Time	Food, Drinks (Circle Meals)	Amount	How Cooked	# Min. Eating	Eating Speed (1-7) 1 = Slow	Hunger Before (1-7) 1 = Low	Where Eaten	Other Activities	Related Mood Before	Related Thoughts, Feelings, Events	Type	# Min. & Amount	Effort (1-7) 1 = Low
8:15 am	Whole Wheat Toast / Sugar Snaps cereal / Raisins / Whole Milk / Coffee / Cream / Orange Drink	2 / 1/2 cup / teaspoon / 1/2 cup / 3 cups / 1/4 cup / 1 glass		15	6 (very fast)	7 (very hungry)	Kitchen table (seated)	Newspaper	Content, rested	At least I started the day off right with a good breakfast. I'm going to watch what I eat today—I really need to lose weight.			
8:40											Walked	25 min (1 mile)	2
10:30	Jelly Doughnut / Coffee / Nondairy creamer	3 / 2 cups / 2 packets		10	7	1	Work Desk	Working	Anxious	Someone brought in those darn doughnuts & I just couldn't resist them. I'm disgusted with myself now! I'll skip lunch to make up for it.			

FIGURE 2.1. A Self-Monitoring Form as It Might Be Filled Out by an Obese Patient.

NAME Chris Coe DAY Thursday 9/15/82

	Eating										Activity		
Time	Food, Drinks (Circle Meals)	Amount	How Cooked	# Min. Eating	Eating Speed (1–7) 1 = Slow	Hunger Before (1–7) 1 = Low	Where Eaten	Other Activities	Related Mood Before	Thoughts, Feelings, Events	Type	# Min. & Amount	Effort (1–7) 1 = Low
3:00	Candy bar Apple	2 1		5	7 4	7	Standing at vending machine	Talking	Bored, restless	I was really hungry & just couldn't wait until dinner			
5:00											Jogged	20 min	4
5:30	Martini Salted Peanuts	2 1 large bowl		30	4	5	Living room couch	Watching T.V.	Restless	I needed something to help me relax			
8:00	Porterhouse steak Potato Sour cream Butter Ice cream	8 oz. 1 2 Tbsp 1 Tbsp 1 large bowl	Broiled Baked	20	6	4	Kitchen table	Talking with family	Depressed	I ate too much today, again! I hate myself when I look in the mirror!			
11:30	Cookies (Choc. Chip)	15							Hopeless	Why not? I blew it anyway.			

GOALS: To reduce my intake of sugar

FIGURE 2.1. A Self-Monitoring Form as It Might Be Filled Out by an Obese Patient (continued).

27

DAILY FOOD RECORD

Day/ Time	Location	With Whom	Degree of Hunger Before Eating (0–10)	If Binge Mark (✓)	Food: Types and Quantity	Activity While Eating	Degree of Fullness After Eating (0–10)	Vomiting (V) Laxatives (L)	Sensation/ Feelings After Vomiting	

FIGURE 2.2. A Self-Monitoring Form for Use with Bulimic Individuals.

Chapter 3
A Treatment Program for Mild to Moderate Obesity

The behavioral treatment of obesity stems from a study by Ferster, Nurnberger, and Levitt that was published in 1962. These authors reasoned that obese eating behavior was largely determined by environmental influences, and they developed a program to enable overweight individuals to exert more control over adverse aspects of their personal food environment. Their clients were advised to eat in only one place with a distinctive place setting, thus narrowing the circumstances under which eating was likely to occur. In addition, Ferster and his colleagues observed that the obese tended to eat their food more quickly than the nonobese, and instituted procedures, such as putting down utensils between bites, to slow the eating rate.

Research has since suggested that some of the assumptions underlying this seminal study were unwarranted. It has been shown that some persons at all weight levels are more sensitive to environmental control of eating than others, suggesting that such sensitivity is not a necessary characteristic of the overweight individual (Rodin et al., 1977). However, the stimulus-control approach advocated by Ferster and his colleagues to narrow the events associated with eating would still be useful even if the obese were not especially sensitive to environmental events. Similarly, as we saw in the last chapter, although some studies have shown that the obese tend to eat more quickly and chew their food less than the nonobese or thin individuals (Adams et al., 1978) other studies have not shown such differences (Stunkard, Coll, Lundquist, & Meyers, 1980).

Although a therapy may be based upon the shaky foundation of questionable assumptions, it may still work. The behavioral treatment of obesity has in fact been shown, in numerous controlled studies, to be superior to no treatment, to various placebo-control conditions, and to more traditional approaches to weight loss such as dietary programs, psychotherapy, and even pharmacologic treatment (Wilson, 1980). The results of treatment are usually modest, with mean losses of some .5 to 1.0 kg per week of treatment. Because treatment usually lasts about 10 weeks, the mean weight loss reported in research studies is 5.0 kg (Wilson, 1980). A recent review of the literature suggests that in the last few years behavioral programs have been extended in length, a change that has been associated with an increase in the mean weight loss achieved to 7.0 kg (Brownell & Wadden, 1986). The variation in weight changes between individuals is large, ranging from small increases in weight to losses of 15 kg. These findings suggest, first, that the behavioral treatment of obesity is most suitable for the mildly overweight and that, second, treatment should be extended beyond the usual 10-week program if weight losses are to exceed the 5.0 kg average noted above. Such extended treatment may be problematic in terms of its affordability. Therefore, although some behavioral treatment programs offer longer treatment packages, others offer maintenance or booster sessions as a separate option. In general, given the above-noted findings concerning the advantage of longer treatment, the participant should be given the expectation that an extended treatment program will yield better results. Thus, maintenance sessions should be built into the basic program.

One explanation for the marked variability in weight loss between individuals might lie in personal differences that affect outcome. Despite an intensive search for such differences, almost no pretreatment characteristics of the obese predict outcome, including: age, sex, age at onset of obesity, number of attempts to lose weight, and measures of externality (Wilson, 1985). It is generally agreed that depression affects outcome, but no studies of this issue have appeared because depressed individuals are usually excluded from weight-reduction studies. Nonetheless, as noted in the previous chapter, it seems reasonable to exclude patients with marked depression or with current life disruptions, as such factors undoubtedly affect compliance with the treatment regimen. Binge eating was shown in one study to predict a poor outcome (Keefe et al., 1984). Special attention to this problem, therefore, would seem to be useful. In addition, patients with obese spouses seem to fare less well than those with non-obese spouses (Dubbert & Wilson, in press). This makes good sense because an obese spouse might model poor eating habits and refuse to modify his/her behavior, making it difficult for the patient to adhere to the weight-loss program. It may be wise to involve obese spouses in the weight-loss program.

Another explanation for variability in outcome might reside in differences in adherence to the treatment program. There is some evidence that patients who do not monitor their eating behavior do less well than those that do (Dubbert & Wilson, 1983). In addition, early failure to lose weight seems to predict a poor outcome. This suggests that individuals who do not lose weight in the first few weeks of treatment should be reevaluated, with the aim of altering the therapeutic program.

Finally, there might be specific elements of a weight-loss program that would tend to produce superior results. One such element is the use of a refundable deposit contingent upon weight loss or upon attendance. The use of such a contingency reduces dropout rates to less than 10% compared with a usual rate of some 20%. In addition, superior results are obtained when refunds of money are made contingent upon weight loss, enhancing the results of the standard program up to 50% (Jeffery, Björnson-Benson, Rosenthal, Kurth, & Dunn, 1984). Another procedure that may hold some promise is the inclusion of spouses in treatment to enhance social support. In the first study of this issue (Brownell, Heckerman, Westlake, Hayes, & Monti, 1978) obese individuals were assigned to one of three groups. Those with cooperative spouses were assigned either to a group with or without spouse involvement; those with uncooperative spouses were assigned to a no-spouse-involvement group. Involvement of the spouse in treatment much enhanced outcome in terms of weight lost (13.5 kg vs. 8.8 kg). Since that time, some studies have replicated the advantage for spouse involvement whereas others have not. Spouses are not routinely involved in weight-loss programs at the present time (Agras & Arnow, in press).

Maintenance of weight loss through behavioral treatment has been shown to be satisfactory to 1-year follow-up. A longer-term follow-up also showed good maintenance for participants who reported continued exercise and who maintained their changes in eating behavior (Graham, Taylor, Hovell, & Siegel, 1983). However, the variance in weight changes between individuals increases as the follow-up period lengthens.

Despite the differences between weight-loss programs in terms of setting and the educational backgrounds of the clinicians involved, the procedures used in behavioral programs are strikingly similar from one center to another. The major elements of the program include:

1. Self-monitoring of eating behavior and activity levels;
2. Instructions to control environmental influences upon eating;
3. Procedures designed to decrease the rate of eating;
4. Alterations in dietary content, reducing fat and alcohol intake and increasing consumption of complex carbohydrates;
5. Increase in structured and unstructured exercise;
6. Contingency management procedures aimed at increasing attendance, and occasionally weight loss; and
7. Attention to cognitive processes that interfere with the necessary behavior changes.

A description of such a program follows.

A BASIC PROGRAM FOR WEIGHT REDUCTION

An outline of the first 8 weeks of a group-based behavioral program for weight reduction is presented in this section. This program can be adapted for use with individual clients (see Wyshograd, 1985). Follow-up sessions, as described in the next chapter, should be added to extend the treatment length to

6 months or more. The aim of the program is to teach specific skills to the participants in a flexible manner, encouraging each participant to select aspects of the program that are most applicable to him or her. In the group mode each session lasts about 90 minutes, or in the case of individuals, between 30 and 50 minutes. Because this is a skills-training program, the sessions are more structured than in the usual group psychotherapy approach. It is essential that the therapist retain leadership of the group throughout treatment, and follow the protocol accurately. No participant should be allowed to monopolize the session. The therapist should encourage group members to share their experiences in a positive manner and in keeping with the theme of each session. Positive communications of this kind should be reinforced by attention from the therapist. Groups with a positive tone tend to lose more weight than those with a negative tone. The therapist should also ensure that each group member has a chance to contribute to each of the sessions.

There has been little research devoted to the optimal sequencing of the various components of behavioral weight-loss programs. The sequencing presented here has been developed in our clinic over the past decade and appears optimal for clients in our setting. Other sequences may work better with different populations in different settings, and the manuals described at the end of this chapter provide a variety of sequences.

Due to space limitations, only the essential points are presented in the following outline of the program. Sections in quotation marks are written as direct communications from the therapist.

Session 1

The aims of the first session are to introduce the program to the participants and to enhance expectations of success in a realistic manner. The goal of gradual weight loss is emphasized and myths about obesity debunked. Common myths include: Overweightness is caused by hormonal problems; obesity is inherited so nothing can be done; exercise increases appetite. The main elements of the program—behavior change, cognitive change, and problem solving—are described. The participant homework assignment for the first week is to self-monitor food intake and to reinforce success using a nonfood reward.

When introducing a new therapy, several procedures may be useful in enhancing the participants' processing of the new information (Rosenthal & Downs, 1985). These include: the provision of facts about the presenting problem and the treatment, a rationale for therapy, previews of the upcoming procedures, and, if available, handouts or a manual for the participant (see end of chapter for examples).

The main rationale for the program is that weight loss can best be accomplished by specific behavior changes that have been documented to be useful in many research studies. Weight loss leads to a number of well-documented health benefits, including lower blood pressure and cholesterol levels with resultant decrease in risk for heart disease, enhanced glucose metabolism and lowered risk for diabetes, and lessened wear and tear on joints and lowered risk for osteoarthritis. The exercise components of the program will also lead to enhanced muscular strength and an increased feeling of well-being.

If the program uses contingencies for weight loss or for attendance, these should of course have been discussed in the assessment session and a written contract developed. Such contingencies are highly recommended. The best method of refunding money contingent upon weight loss appears to be an increasing incentive for successive increments of weight loss (Jeffery et al., 1984). In the latter study, $5, $10, $20, $40, and $75 were refunded for each incremental weight loss of 5 lbs in a 16-week program.

Behavior Change. "Behavior is influenced by things and people in the immediate environment; many people eat because food is available and in sight, rather than because they are hungry, or because others insist upon it either at home, in restaurants, or at parties. The good side of this is that you can gain more control of your environment.

The behaviors to be changed during the course of this program include activity levels, food selections, and eating style (for example, slowing the speed of eating). Altering environmental factors influencing eating behavior is another change. These behavior changes are central to the program, and if carried out thoroughly should lead to weight loss."

Changing Cognitions. "What goes on in our minds also influences our behavior, often by discouraging necessary behavior changes. Among these influences are: expectations, beliefs, thoughts, perceptions of self, self-talk, and our confidence in achieving our goals. Too little confidence can lead to failure, often because inappropriately high or distant goals are set. Nothing induces confidence like success, so set small goals that can be accomplished in a day or 2. Examples of counterproductive thoughts include: being impatient at the recommended slow rate of weight loss—remember that slow is better in the long run; guilt or depression about failures; obsessive dwelling upon food; thinking you lack willpower; comparing yourself with someone who is thinner, or who is losing weight faster; giving up trying to make changes because of one mistake."

Problem Solving. "No one is in a better position to identify and resolve your weight problems than yourself. Everyone is unique, and there are many different ingredients that lead to a particular weight problem. You will need to identify your own difficulties during this course. Some people, for example, eat too much fat; others may eat too many sweets, or big meals, or eat no regular meals but just nibble; others may be inactive. Any of these difficulties, singly or in combination, or others may be contributing to your particular problem. With proper training anyone can identify their problem areas and work to change them. You can also identify your strengths and work to enhance them.

A major goal of this program is to help you become your own therapist, a personal scientist able to identify and solve your own weight-control problems. There is no magic solution, as most of you already know. You will be successful in your efforts to the extent that you take charge of your own program. We are here to help you. It is like learning to drive. At first someone sits beside you to help out if you make mistakes. But to become a good driver you have to practice driving, and, ultimately drive on your own.

To solve your own problems you will learn to: monitor your behavior so that you become aware of problem areas, make effective commitments to change by setting small realistic goals, drawing up contracts to help achieve goals, and rewarding yourself when you make changes."

Monitoring Behavior. The therapist should now ask the participants to take out the food/activity record sample and blanks (see Figure 2.1 for an example of such a form). "Because self-diagnosis is the cornerstone for behavior change, it should come as no surprise that the most successful participants in this program are those who regularly and accurately monitor their behavior. Besides self-diagnosis, record keeping allows the identification of behaviors that can be changed, and also highlights areas of strength and progress."

Setting Goals. The therapist should now ask the participants to take out the personal goal sheet (Figure 3.1). "The purpose of this form is to help set clear and attainable goals each week. This week the goal is self-monitoring. You should think how many days it will be realistic for you to self-monitor, given your other commitments. Write down in the other goals column 'keep record for (number of) days.' Remember that record keeping is most important, so the more days you can do it, the better. On the other hand, we want you to begin to be realistic about the changes you can make in order to enhance success and minimize failure."

Self-Reward. The therapist should now ask the participants to think about possible rewards for successful behavior change. "A reward for making the change will help ensure that you will continue. There are some rules: The reward must not be a food item; the reward should only be given on meeting the goal; the reward should occur very soon after meeting the goal." The therapist should now ask the participants to fill in a reward to be used after meeting the goal for the first 6 days of this week.

In closing, the therapist should remind the participants that they know a good deal about themselves and about weight loss already, so that they should put some of that knowledge to use during the coming week, to ensure a good start on the road to success. A demonstration of walking as an exercise will be held before the next session. Interested participants should be instructed to arrive 20 minutes before the session begins.

PERSONAL GOAL SHEET FOR _____ (attach to food record)

	FOOD, EATING & ENVIRONMENTAL GOALS			AEROBIC ACTIVITY GOALS				OTHER ACTIVITY GOALS			OTHER GOALS			
Date	Goal	Times/ Week	Rate 1–5	Type	# min	Times/ Week	Rate 1–5	Type	Times/ Week	Rate 1–5	Goal	Times/ Week	Rate 1–5	Total

FIGURE 3.1. A Form on Which Obese Individuals Can Note Their Personal Goals During the Course of Weight-Reduction Therapy.

Session 2

The main aims of this session are to review the food records and the use of a nonfood reward for success, to review the participants' activity levels, and to introduce the topic of increasing both structured and unstructured activity. In each session certain teaching techniques may prove useful. These include summarizing the main points to be covered at the beginning of each session, using modeling, that is, demonstrating a behavior change, and using concrete examples from successful participants to illustrate particular points. About 20 minutes before the session the therapist should meet with those participants who elected to come early. He/she should demonstrate and have the participants practice strolling, ordinary walking, and brisk walking. The sedentary should be reminded that they must begin with ordinary walking and work up to brisk walking.

At each of the sessions participants should report a few minutes before the session begins so they can be weighed. This provides an opportunity for a brief personal interaction between the therapist and participant. Progress in terms of weight reduction should be praised appropriately, however, the therapist should note that the behaviors being changed are as important as weight loss in the first few sessions. This can be used to encourage the participant who does not lose weight, and can form an area for review by the participant. Participants should be taught how to plot their weight on a graph.

The first portion of *every* session should highlight the topic for the week, and then focus on the homework given the week before, including the self-monitoring of critical behaviors and compliance with any behavior-change prescription. In the second portion of each session new material is introduced and discussed.

Enhancing Activity. As an introduction to the topic of enhancing activity, several points should be emphasized. Restriction of diet, although useful in weight loss, is largely offset over a relatively brief length of time by a reduction in basal metabolic rate, that is, the rate at which calories are burned to fuel the body. This accounts for the plateau so often encountered in weight loss. Exercise increases metabolic rate, thus helping to eliminate the plateau. However, such increases last only for 24 hours, so there is a need for a *daily* activity program. A further benefit is that moderate increases in activity are associated with a decrease in appetite for many individuals.

Beyond the benefits for weight loss, increased activity has important physiological benefits, including improved cardiovascular and pulmonary functioning and muscle strength; as well as psychological benefits, including diminished stress responses; and reductions in anxiety and depression. These are important side benefits of this program. There are two main categories of activity, unstructured daily activities, and planned aerobic activities.

Unstructured Activity. These include walking up and down stairs instead of using an elevator or escalator, parking far away from a building, and eliminating extension telephones to help increase walking at home.

Structured Aerobic Activity. The ultimate goal of the program is 30 minutes of vigorous aerobic exercise 6 or 7 days a week. This frequency is important to continually enhance basal metabolic rate. However, for maintenance and for cardiovascular conditioning, a rate of 4 times a week will suffice. It is important to consider what frequency and time will best fit into one's life, because to be maintained exercise must be feasible. For many people the easiest and most effective exercise is brisk walking. Other exercises include swimming, jogging, cycling, either indoors or outside, and calisthenics. It is important to emphasize that this level of exercise should be built up gradually to avoid aching muscles and potential injury. In building up the exercise program several dimensions can be varied, including frequency, duration, and intensity. Several practical aspects of exercise should be considered, such as wearing the right clothing and shoes and doing stretching exercises to warm up and to cool down. A demonstration of some simple stretching exercises may be useful.

The session should end with a personal goal setting for the next week, which should include continued self-monitoring, making changes in unstructured and structured exercise, and using self-reinforcement for successful changes.

Session 3

The aims of this session are to review compliance with the activities contracted for during the last session, namely self-monitoring, the participants' changes in activity levels, and the use of self-reinforcement. Difficulties in adherence to the instructions should be carefully addressed using a problem-solving approach. Finally, the topic of beginning to change the personal food environment and eating style should be introduced. Barriers to change should be examined and dealt with. It is helpful to have participants list such barriers, including excuses for not exercising, and have other group members refute them. In this way some of the cognitive distortions of each participant can be challenged.

Introduction of Changes in the Personal Food Environment and Eating Style. The therapist should now introduce the rationale for making changes in eating style. "As we have seen, the environment controls much of our behavior. While there are bad aspects of this, that is, we can sometimes feel at the mercy of an adverse environment, the good aspect is that we can control our personal environment to a large extent. From the viewpoint of eating behavior, certain things become signals to eat even though we may not be hungry. Of these the most important is the sight of food. Thus, one of the first things to do is to inspect

your homes and remove all food from sight. This might include removing tempting snack food stored in cupboards.

Along the same lines it is important to eat *only* when you are sitting down at a
table and with a table setting. If you often eat in front of the TV set, turning on
the TV will become a signal to snack. Eating while doing other things also
means that you are not attending to the pleasurable aspects of eating. Switch off
the TV and notice how much you are not noticing.

The way in which you eat is also important. Studies have shown that the
obese tend to take bigger bites, eat their food more quickly, and chew it less well
than those of normal weight. This 'obese eating style' can be detected as early as
18 months of age. So it is important to slow down eating rate, to take smaller
bites, and to chew your food well."

The therapist should now distribute a piece of food (for example fruit, a vegetable such as celery sticks, low-fat nonsalt potato chips, etc.) to each participant, asking them first to jot down as many adjectives as they can to describe
the food in terms of appearance, smell, taste, texture, and temperature. The
goal of this exercise is to increase perception regarding food as it is eaten,
encouraging people to savor each morsel of food. Then the participants should
take another piece of food and determine how many chews it takes to liquify the
food. It should be pointed out to participants that all food should be chewed in
this way, all the time.

Finally, exercise should be discussed with the group in terms of its implications for home use, barriers to change, etc. It should be pointed out that a 5-year
follow-up study (Graham et al., 1983) found that the participants who continued an exercise program, and who continued to make the changes in eating
style, showed excellent maintenance of weight loss and even some continued
weight loss over a 5-year period. Those not continuing these practices showed
weight gain. The therapist should note that we are not sure how such eating style
changes work in terms of weight loss. Possibilities are that the slow style leads to
less caloric intake, or that the slow style leads to longer lasting satiation, a propo-
sition for which there is some experimental evidence.

Goals should now be set for the next week, including self-monitoring, extension of the exercise program, changing stimulus control and eating style, and
using self-reward.

Session 4

The aims of this session are: (a) to review and extend the behavior changes
being made by the participants in regard to activity levels and eating behavior
using group participation and ingenuity to solve problems; and (b) to introduce
the topic of more healthy food choices, in particular reducing the intake of saturated fats (the sort that are solid at room temperature).

Fats. Adopting a diet lower in saturated fat has two advantages that should be pointed out to participants. First, fats are dense in calories, hence, by eating less fat and more complex carbohydrates (vegetables and breads are lower in caloric density and should be substituted for fat — this will be addressed in detail in the next session), the caloric composition of the diet can be reduced without increasing appetite. *Fats* are 9 calories/g; *Carbohydrates* are 4 calories/g; *Protein* is 4 calories/g; *Alcohol* is 7 calories/g. Second, high cholesterol levels are a prime risk factor for coronary heart disease. By reducing saturated fats, these levels can be reduced. As with all other behavior changes, the principle of gradualism should be used, particularly because other family members should be involved in this dietary change to improve their health and because we are aiming at long-term alterations in diet.

Among the healthful dietary changes to be made in the area of fats are:

1. Reduce weekly servings of whole milk, cheese (other than low-fat cottage cheese), fatty meats (beef, lamb, bacon, spareribs, sausage, and luncheon meats), and ice cream by one half (e.g., from the U.S. average of 24 servings a week to about 12 per week). Substitute complex carbohydrate foods and foods such as fish and poultry in their place. (Do not eat chicken skin.)
2. Change from ice cream to ice milk and from whole milk to nonfat milk.
3. Reduce meat fat by trimming and by broiling or roasting instead of frying.
4. Eliminate, except for rare use, intake of organ meats such as liver, sweetbreads, and brains.
5. Change from butter or hard margarine (made with hydrogenated oil) to soft tub margarine (made with unhydrogenated oil).
6. Change from lard or shortening to unhydrogenated vegetable oil, including olive oil if desired. Any type of vegetable oil other than palm or coconut oil is acceptable. (Healthy cultures have successfully used olive oil, a monosaturated oil, for thousands of years.) Avoid use of large amounts of vegetable oils, as you want to lower your total fat intake in Phase 1 from the current U.S. average of 40% to about 30% of total calories consumed.
7. Reduce consumption of egg yolks to no more than four a week. Use egg whites liberally.
8. Change from creamy peanut butter made with hydrogenated fat to natural peanut butter without hydrogenated fat.
9. Reduce consumption of fast foods, processed and convenience foods, commercial baked goods, and the like.

Handouts of educational material on "heart-healthy diets" are useful at this stage. The therapist should have the participants take out their current food logs and assess, by circling the fat-containing food items, where the sources of fat in their own diets come from. Participants should begin to work out substitutes for high-fat foods. The group should be encouraged to continue this analysis at home. This should lead to a general discussion of sources and options for change, for example, removing fat from meats, eating more fish and poultry, using more vegetables and a lower proportion of meats in their meals.

Alcohol intake should also be reduced, because alcohol provides "empty" nonnutritious calories. Drinking two cans of regular beer each day provides enough calories for a weight gain of over 30 lb a year. Cutting down on alcohol is an easy way to reduce caloric intake without increasing hunger. In addition, if alcohol is reduced it is less easy to lose control over eating because the temptation to eat a little more often occurs after a drink or two, a time when self-control has been weakened by the alcohol intake.

The new goal for the week is to begin changes toward a healthier diet by beginning to reduce fat, and alcohol intake.

Session 5

The main aims of this session are to review the participants' progress in changing exercise habits, eating behavior, and in modifying fat intake. In addition, a general review of weight loss to date should be made, because poor responders to the program may need individual attention, the addition of fenfluramine, or a very-low-calorie diet. Finally, the topic of dietary content, namely, the increased use of complex carbohydrates, is addressed.

Overview of Progress. To begin the session, the group leader should ask the participants to take out their weight-loss graphs and review them. An example of such a graph is shown in Figure 3.2. Weight losses should ideally fall between the average and maximum change lines, for this session between 3 and 6 lbs. If weight losses do not fall between these figures then there is a problem. Participants should be asked to decide: (a) Do they have a problem with weight loss? (The therapist might ask for a show of hands); and (b) If they do, what is likely to be causing the problem? The most usual cause is that not enough behavior change has been made. Changes need to be made in all the areas, including exercise, eating behavior, and nutritional changes (which will be expanded on in today's session). Individual problems should be identified and arrangements for an individual session to explore such problems further should be made if necessary.

The problems noted by participants are quite varied and are usually concerned with deficient compliance to the program instructions. Inadequate self-monitoring is a frequent cause of poor weight loss because the areas requiring change are not adequately addressed and the participant does not receive adequate feedback concerning the changes made. Problems with self-monitoring may reflect a low priority given to weight loss by the participant. This needs to be discussed in detail, and if the priorities cannot be changed it may be better to counsel the patient that this is a poor time, given the competing demands on

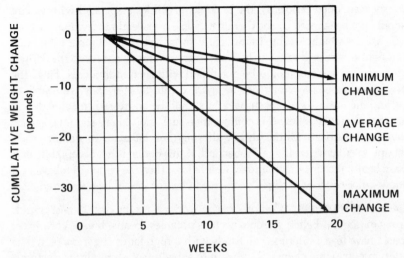

FIGURE 3.2. A Sample Graph Indicating Minimum, Average, and Maximum Expected Weight Losses for a Behavior Therapy Program.

time, to attempt to lose weight. If the patient can give an adequate priority to the weight-loss program and to self-monitoring, then a shaping approach may be needed, starting with 2 or 3 days a week and slowly increasing the frequency.

Insufficient exercise is another frequently encountered problem at this point in therapy. Exercise may be scheduled too infrequently, again perhaps a question of priorities, or it may be of insufficient duration or of insufficient intensity. Each of these possibilities requires investigation. The feasibility of the needed changes should be discussed with the participant and a plan worked out to attain the necessary exercise levels. Another problem may be poor nutrition, especially the continued consumption of high-fat foods or large amounts of sweetened foods. The latter problem may be accompanied by binge eating. The obese binge eater tends to have the same pattern of food intake as the bulimic, namely, inadequate amounts of food for breakfast and lunch, leading to feelings of hunger by midafternoon followed by binge eating. Individual counseling may be needed to help overcome these eating patterns, in which case the format for the first half-dozen sessions of the bulimia protocol described in chapter 5 should be followed. In some cases of binge eating, as described in the following chapter, the use of low-dosage fenfluramine may be useful.

Finally, interpersonal problems, for example with a spouse, or life stresses that may not have been apparent at initial assessment may be interfering with weight loss. Such problems should be carefully examined in an individual session, and a decision made as to whether weight-loss therapy should be continued and whether counseling regarding the particular problem should be instituted.

Although the most frequent cause of a failure to lose weight will be one of the previously mentioned problems, the biological realities associated with weight loss should not be ignored by the therapist. Some overweight individuals defend strongly against weight loss by dramatically lowering basal metabolic rate. Such persons may adhere well to a weight-loss program yet may not attain the desired weight loss. Two options should be examined with such individuals. First, the question of whether they may not be more comfortable if they were able to accept and maintain their present weight should be addressed in some detail. Should they decide to follow this course, then such individuals should continue to attend the sessions with the aim of altering their behavior to stabilize their weight and to enhance their health. Second, if this option is not acceptable, or if there are health reasons that mandate weight loss, then the option of following a very-low-calorie diet as outlined in the next chapter should be considered.

Complex Carbohydrates. "Complex carbohydrates are the dieter's best friend. Contrary to popular belief, starches such as potatoes, beans, bread, corn, rice, and pasta have fewer calories than foods with a high fat or sugar content. The next step in nutritional change is to begin to substitute such foods for the foods high in fat, thus reducing the caloric intake without deprivation, and reducing cholesterol intake for a more heart-healthy diet. There are other health benefits such as a reduction in constipation, and possibly some protection against cancer of the colon." The following are suggestions concerning increasing the use of complex carbohydrates.

1. Increase intake of complex carbohydrate foods—including legumes (e.g., beans, peas, lentils), starchy root vegetables such as the potato, and other vegetables and fruits—as a partial caloric replacement for reduced intake of sugar and fatty animal foods.
2. Gradually introduce lightly milled or whole-grained cereals into your food plan (e.g., whole-wheat bread and flour, bulgur, couscous, cracked wheat, rolled oats, rye, brown rice, etc.).
3. Increase intake of whole fruits (fruit juices lack much of the fiber contained in whole fruits).
4. Increase intake of whole vegetables (vegetable juices lack much of the fiber contained in whole vegetables and often contain significant amounts of added salt).

Sugar Control. Simple sugars can insidiously add calories to the diet. The following are ways to help cut down on consumption of such edibles.

1. Reduce consumption of soft drinks by at least one half. Limit intake to two or three a week. (U.S. average is five 12-ounce cans or bottles a week.) Switch to (low salt) bottled water instead.
2. Gradually eliminate the use of sugar in coffee or tea and on fruit. (Saccharin use is discouraged, not only because of its possible role as a carcinogen but also because of the importance of retraining your palate to lowered sweetness levels.)

3. Switch from heavy to light syrup in canned fruits, and eventually substitute fresh fruits for the canned variety.
4. Substitute fresh fruit for pastry, cake, pie, or other sweets in one third of all desserts to begin with, gradually increasing to 90%.

Sometimes participants will ask about cookbooks that provide recipes that are in line with the program. The following have been found to be useful:

American Heart Association Cookbook. New York: Ballantine Books. Paperback $3.95.
Recipes for a Small Planet. Ellen B. Ewald. New York: Ballantine Books. Paperback $3.95.
The Living Heart Diet. Michael DeBakey, Antonio M. Gotto, Lynne W. Scott, John P. Foreyt. New York: Raven Press. Hardcover $9.95.

Session 6

This session has the following aims: to review progress in exercise, eating behavior, and nutritional changes. At this point most participants should be consolidating the behavior changes they are making, and this session should deal with residual problems concerning these changes. During this session, participants will examine the environmental control of stimuli concerned with food consumption and flesh out the nutritional information with advice concerning salt- and caffeine-containing foods. This information is generally useful for maintenance of health and because some obese individuals have fluctuating weights due to fluid retention based upon high and varying sodium intakes.

Environmental Control. This section might start with the therapist reminding participants that they can control a major part of their personal food environment by reducing the number and type of food signals. These food cues prompt eating behavior, much of which is unnecessary or excessive. There are three main elements that can be changed, some of which have been briefly alluded to previously.

1. Removing high-calorie foods from the personal environment.
2. Separating eating from other activities.
3. Reducing food servings and using smaller plates.

The therapist should present specific examples in each of these areas and promote group discussion about potential changes, reminding participants that they should add one or more of these changes to this week's contract.

Planning food intake for the day can also be a very useful method of gaining control over the food environment. Here, the notion of three adequate meals with good food content should be the goal. Planning food buying ahead of time and working from a shopping list so as to resist the impulse to buy other foods is also useful. Shopping at a time when one is not hungry is undoubtedly preferable to shopping for food when hungry.

Lowering Salt and Caffeine Intake. A handout on the salt content of various foods should be provided at this point. "The most obvious way to reduce salt intake is to avoid the use of the salt shaker at the table and in cooking. In addition, there are a number of foods that are particularly high in sodium that should be avoided, and those medium in sodium that should be reduced as follows:

1. Eliminate, except for rare use, high-salt items such as bacon, ham, sausage, frankfurters, luncheon meats, salted nuts, sauerkraut, pickles, canned soups, canned vegetables, potato chips, and other salted snack foods.
2. Switch from regular table salt to a light salt (one-half sodium chloride, one-half potassium chloride).
3. Gradually decrease salt use in cooking to about one third of previous levels; simultaneously decrease, and eventually eliminate, salt use at the table.
4. Explore the use of other flavors in your cooking—spices, herbs, lemon, wine, vinegar, etc.
5. Limit intake of caffeinated drinks (coffee, tea, cola, etc.) to 4 cups a day at first and then to 2 cups. Try decaffeinated alternatives and herb teas."

Session 7

The aims of this session are to review and continue to consolidate the changes made in exercise, eating style, nutrition, and environmental cues leading to eating, and to introduce the participants to the role of cognitions in maintaining faulty eating or exercise patterns.

Effect of the Social Environment on Food Consumption. "Eating is often a social event, and at such events various cues may prompt you to eat things you don't really want. For example, the sight of others eating is a powerful cue to join in. Taking the case of a party or an office picnic, there are a number of things you can do, provided you plan ahead. These include:

1. Planning your caloric consumption that day to allow for the extra calories. However, this should not lead to missing meals that day, rather, the amount eaten at each meal should be reduced.
2. You can plan to eat smaller portions of the high-calorie foods at the picnic or party.
3. You can choose appropriate foods from those served at the party or picnic, limiting yourself to foods high in starch and fiber, and avoiding the fatty foods, red meats, etc. At nearly all parties or picnics there are a variety of salads, breads, chicken, turkey, etc." This alternative is the most appropriate, and therefore the one to work towards.

Cognitive Ecology. "Discouragement is a major problem for those trying to improve their health by losing weight. Often such discouragement arises from things we say to ourselves, or from expectations or beliefs that are unrealistic. It is important to challenge faulty self-talk, expectations, and beliefs, and to sub-stitute more accurate expectations and supportive rather than destructive self-talk. There are several things you can do to make positive changes:"

1. *Identify your faulty expectations.* "Do you expect to lose weight without making changes in your behavior? Do you expect these changes to be only temporary? Do you expect to lose weight more quickly than you are doing? Do you expect to lose weight without any setbacks? All these may be exam-ples of faulty expectations. It is important to identify the expectations that you keep at the back of your mind, and to bring them into line with reality ."
2. *Identify negative self-talk, and substitute positive statements.* "Such state-ments include: 'This will never work. I've tried hard and haven't lost any-thing.' 'I've starved all day. Now I deserve some treats'. 'I'm just too busy right now to change my eating patterns'. Such thoughts should be challenged and more positive thoughts substituted."
3. *Reward positive behaviors.* The group should be reminded that self-reward can strengthen behavior change by enhancing motivation and making one feel good about achievements. The reward plan should be designed with the following features in mind:
   (a) "Plan rewards that are reasonably easy to achieve, and that you will enjoy. Give yourself the reward only when the behavior has been accom-plished, for example, brisk walking for 35 minutes for 5 days in a week. Give yourself the reward very soon after the behavior has been accom-plished. Then plan the next behavioral sequence that you want to reward." The participants should be reminded that they may have to use something that they would ordinarily have access to as a reward, by allowing themselves to have it only when the behavior to be reinforced has been accomplished.
   (b) The reward should be enjoyable and should not be food.
   (c) Positive self-statements are free and are reinforcing. Participants should be encouraged to use self-praise for accomplishments.

Session 8

The main aims of this session are to further consolidate the behavior changes being made by participants, to solve residual problems, and to continue to explore cognitive emotional barriers to change. Toward the end of the session the question of maintenance should be broached and the participants asked to con-sider between now and the next session whether they would like to attend main-tenance sessions. As discussed earlier, an alternative approach is to include such sessions as part of the treatment package extending treatment to 16 sessions or more.

Cognitive Ecology. To begin this part of the session, the participants should be asked about the patterns of thinking (about food, exercise, nutrition, or weight loss) that they have observed in themselves since the last session, and whether such patterns were positive or negative in their influence. If cognitions were counterproductive, what changes were made toward more positive thinking? This should lead to a general group discussion, sharing of experience, and problem solving. Distorted cognitions should be discussed and methods of challenging them and substituting more adaptive cognitions should be sought through group discussion.

A useful additional area to address is the question of the response of key individuals in the participants' environment to both the efforts they are making toward losing weight, and the weight loss itself. Examples of responses, both positive and negative, should be sought from the group, and methods of dealing with negative responses (i.e., not responding) should be discussed. In addition, the participants should be asked to consider ways in which they might elicit positive responses from key individuals.

Problem-Solving Review. Most of this session should be concerned with a review of progress to date and with the identification of residual problems. To facilitate this, the Problem-Solving Checklist found in Appendix B should be handed out to the group. This checklist provides a systematic review of each area of behavior change to help participants identify current problems. It also provides a systematic approach to devising a suitable intervention and for assessing the effects of the intervention. The group should be encouraged to share problems in each of the behavior-change areas and to help brainstorm potential solutions.

Suggested Additional Reading. Fat is a Feminist Issue. Susie Orbach. New York: Berkley Books. Paperback $3.50. Many participants have found this to be an interesting and informative book that fits in well with the sessions on cognitive ecology.

WEIGHT-LOSS MANUALS

The Learn Program for Weight Control. Kelly D. Brownell, PhD

This is a nicely produced bound paperback manual intended for use by the participant. Sixteen lessons are presented, together with a number of appendices, including a calorie guide. "Learn" is an acronym for: Lifestyle, Exercise, Attitudes, Relationships, and Nutrition. The manual provides a detailed guide to the participant to make behavior changes in each of these important areas.

The manual is over 200 pages in length and costs $15.00. Orders or inquiries should be directed to: Kelly D. Brownell, PhD, Department of Psychiatry, University of Pennsylvania, 133 South 36th Street, Philadelphia, PA 19104. Checks should be made out to Dr. Kelly Brownell.

Weight Participant Manual. Robert W. Jeffery, PhD

This is a participant's manual, originally designed for weight loss with hypertensive individuals, but easily adaptable to any person desiring a moderate weight loss by removing the first three pages. Twelve lessons are presented, covering the major behavior change areas, as well as maintenance planning.

The manual is 66 pages in length and costs $11.95 for a paper copy, or $5.95 for a microfiche. It is obtainable from: National Technical Information Service, U.S. Department of Commerce, 5285 Port Royal Road, Springfield, VA 22161. When ordering, quote the NTIS Accession Number PB 8-6-111184/AS and request "HPT Participant Manual—Weight."

Home Correspondence Weight Control Manual. Robert W. Jeffery, PhD

This is a participants' manual designed for the Minneapolis MRFIT Program for use as a home-based correspondence course for those desiring to lose weight. It again covers the major areas involved in a behavioral approach to weight loss, and may be very useful as patient handouts supplementing a program such as the one described in this chapter. Nine sessions are presented in this manual.

The manual is 52 pages in length and costs $10 per copy. It is obtainable from: Robert W. Jeffery, PhD, Division of Epidemiology, School of Public Health, University of Minnesota, Stadium Gate 27, 611 Beacon Street S.E., Minneapolis, MN 55455.

Chapter 4
Extending the Basic Program

As noted in the earlier chapters of this book, there are two potential problems with the behavioral approach to weight loss. The initial weight loss may not be large enough to benefit the client, and the weight loss achieved in the initial period of therapy may not be maintained. Promising solutions to each of these problems are now beginning to become apparent and will form the focus of this chapter. Two approaches have shown some promise in enhancing weight loss: the use of anorectic drugs such as fenfluramine, and the use of a very-low-calorie diet. Maintenance procedures have been devised to extend the results of behavior-change programs through time. Finally, new computerized approaches to weight loss, which take advantage of the clear-cut therapeutic procedures used in the behavioral approach to weight loss, offer increased accessibility of treatment to the client and a lower cost of therapy, and hence may enhance both initial weight loss and the maintenance of such losses.

A BEHAVIORAL APPROACH
TO MAINTENANCE

The main skills involved in maintaining weight losses are:

1. Early identification of problems, especially the regaining of weight.
2. Adequate approaches to problem solving.
3. Successful institution of the solutions discovered in the course of problem solving.
4. Evaluation of the results.

These skills were taught to some extent during the initial eight sessions of the program. In the last session of the program and in the maintenance sessions these skills are particularly emphasized.

Session 9

The main aims of this session are to review progress in the various behavior change areas and continue to have the participants take on greater responsibility for problem solving and goal setting in each of the areas; to present information on relapse prevention, focusing upon an early warning system; and to finalize plans for those who wish to join a maintenance group.

Problem-Solving Review. The group leader should introduce this part of the session by reminding the participants that they have now learned the basic elements of the program, and that the task ahead is to continue to apply what they have learned, in order to extend their weight losses and enhance their health. The first part of the session will be devoted to a review of the various areas for change using a weight-loss activity checklist (Figure 4.1). The checklist should be handed out to the participants and after answering any questions that participants may ask about it, the therapist should suggest that the participants fill out the checklist using their behavior during the last week to report on.

Following completion of the checklist, the group should be encouraged to discuss residual problem areas, and then to devise appropriate interventions. In this exercise the group should be challenged to come up with their own solutions to the problems identified, and the potential advantages and disadvantages of each solution should be discussed. The therapist should ensure that each area of behavior change is discussed by the group.

It is often useful at this point to outline a more formal problem-solving strategy to the participants. This includes the following steps: First, identifying the problem in concrete behavioral terms; second, listing all the possible solutions to the problem; third, ranking the various solutions for practicality; fourth, settling on a particular solution and detailing it; and fifth, making a written contract to implement the solution. This problem-solving method should be used whenever it seems appropriate, and is an important aspect of the maintenance program.

The method of visualizing situations that present a high risk for relapse should also be described to the group, and they should be encouraged to try it out along with visualization of solutions to the problem. When teaching this method, it is useful to demonstrate the procedure with one of the participants, or to model the procedure while describing it aloud. The gradual enhancement of imagery should be demonstrated by adding components from each of the senses in turn, beginning with vision, adding color, smells, sounds, temperature and other sensations, and body sensations from standing, sitting, and moving. Such visualization, because it entails a more detailed approach to the problem, allows for identification of a wider range of potential problems and solutions, and for a better assessment of the probability of success or failure.

NAME _____ DATE _____

WEIGHT LOSS ACTIVITY CHECKLIST

A number of activities related to weight loss are listed below. Think back over the
past week, excluding today. For each activity, place a check mark in each box
corresponding to a day on which you did that activity.

ACTIVITY	MON	TUES	WED	THURS	FRI	SAT	SUN
1. Kept a food record							
2. Kept an activity record							
3. Substituted fish, skinless poultry, vegetables, legumes, for red meat at one or more meals							
4. Limited intake of fats to 2 table-spoons in total of butter, marga-rine, mayonnaise, oil, etc.							
5. Exercised aerobically for at least 20 minutes at a time							
6. Substituted low-fat cheeses such as low-fat cottage cheese, partially skimmed mozzarella and ricotta cheese, for other cheeses							
7. Ate a nutritious breakfast							
8. Ate at least 3 meals at regular times							
9. Substituted low-calorie snacks for high-calorie ones							
10. Chewed food thoroughly at most meals							
11. Ate slowly at most meals							
12. Ate snacks at planned times only							
13. Handled negative feelings such as anger, boredom, tension, etc., by doing something other than eating							
14. Limited alcoholic intake to no more than a glass of wine or light beer							
15. Limited eating to a few appropriate places such as the kitchen table or the cafeteria at work							
16. Sat down for meals							
17. Kept problematic high-calorie foods out of sight							

FIGURE 4.1. A Checklist to Help Participants Review the Behavior Changes That They Have Made
During the Course of Treatment.

When addressing the area of cognitive ecology, the therapist should focus on successes in identifying and challenging negative thoughts concerning weight loss and the necessary behavior changes, and on any environmental impediments to behavior change and weight loss.

Dealing with Setbacks. "Backsliding is inevitable in a weight control program, for example, eating too much in a restaurant, or not exercising for a few days when the weather is bad. But the reaction to such events can be even worse. Faced with this kind of situation, many people resort to catastrophic thinking, feeling that all is lost. This kind of reaction leads inevitably to giving up the program and to total relapse. Instead, view such situations as an opportunity for problem solving along the lines that we have been following for the last few minutes." This notion should be discussed by the group, participants being prompted to give examples of this kind of reaction from their own experience.

Relapse Identification. This section of the session should be introduced by reminding the participants: "As is clear from our discussion today, you have learned the basic elements in a program of weight control and have made many of the necessary behavior changes." From now on participants should extend the behavior changes until they are complete in all areas. The next step is to devise a method to warn that relapse is occurring.

There are two levels of self-observation in this process. The first consists of self-monitoring the key behaviors needed for the participant to lose further weight, or to maintain weight losses. These include exercise, eating behaviors, and control of dietary content. The second consists of observing the end result of these behavior changes, namely weight loss. It should be suggested that participants self-monitor the key behaviors for a few days each month, and compare the results of such self-monitoring with a "good" week during the initial series of weight-loss sessions, or with a goal list that they have constructed for themselves. If problems are detected, participants should be encouraged to use their problem-solving skills to rectify the behavioral deficits, and to write down specific contracts for the next week, continuing to self-monitor the necessary behaviors.

Participants should also be encouraged to weigh themselves at the same time each day once a week, and to plot their weight on a graph. A weight gain of 3 lbs or more that persists longer than 2 weeks is a danger signal. At that point the participant should reinstate self-monitoring and begin to write out a weekly contract for the necessary corrective activities. Obviously the most important areas to survey are the amount and composition of food selection and exercise: Have fats and alcohol crept back into the diet? Or snacks? Has regular exercise disappeared? If weight continues in the danger area despite efforts to change, the participant should call his or her therapist and join a maintenance group or consider retaking the basic course.

"Unlike the traditional diet program—which one starts and goes off—this program has no beginning and no end. The suggested behavior changes need to be made as permanent a part of life as possible, useful not only from the viewpoint of weight loss, but also from the perspective of enhanced health. Thus, one need never consider oneself a failure; aspects of the behavior-change program can be reinstated at any time." The group might then be reminded once more of the findings of the 5-year follow-up of the participants in a weight-loss program (Graham et al., 1983). Those who continued the behavior changes in both eating behavior and activity had lost the most weight at 5 years follow-up. Those who continued one of the areas of change did next best; whereas those who had dropped the behaviors altogether had put on weight. Participants should also be reminded that stabilizing weight is a useful preventive measure; simply stopping the relentless increase in weight that occurs with increasing age will help prevent worsening of some of the risk factors for poor health, such as increased blood pressure, increased cholesterol levels, and abnormal glucose metabolism.

Follow-Up Sessions

Although the usefulness of follow-up sessions in helping participants to maintain their weight loss has not been firmly established in the weight-control literature, it appears that sessions focusing upon problem solving and specific skills training, and providing continued social support, may be useful in maintaining weight losses. As noted in the previous chapter, extending the length of treatment seems to be associated with larger weight losses. Because it has been our experience that no more than half the participants enrolled in a behavioral weight-loss program will decide to attend follow-up sessions (often the participants who lost the most weight during the courses) we would suggest that these sessions should be built into the basic program.

The overall aim of follow-up sessions is to provide a framework for reviewing progress in maintaining the expected behavior changes and consolidating the teaching of problem-solving skills. The frequency of these sessions might be at 2-week intervals at first and then monthly intervals. Longer intervals than 1 month seem to result in poor attendance.

Beginning the Session. The therapist should begin the session by indicating that this is a time to review progress and to solve any problems that are impeding the behavior changes necessary for weight loss. The group leader should then hand out the weight loss activity checklist (Figure 4.1) and ask the group members to take a few moments to fill it out. When this has been accomplished the Problem-Solving Checklist (see Appendix B) should be handed out as a basis for further analysis of problems. The participants should be given a few minutes to read the handout, being told that they will be asked to fill it out as each area of behavior change is reviewed.

Exercise Review. Using the Activity Checklist as a database, the therapist should now ask individuals to fill out the Problem-Solving Checklist for exercise, reminding them that at least 5 days of vigorous activity should be the aim of all participants, for example, 30–40 minutes brisk walking each day or comparable time/effort spent in other structured activities. The role of increasing unstructured activity should also be stressed, because such activities can help to burn calories and maintain health. Individuals should be asked to report on problems identified in this area, and the problem-solving procedure should be outlined and practiced with appropriate group input. Those with problems should be asked whether they have been continuing to keep activity logs on at least an occasional basis, and the suggestion should be made that such logs should be reinstated as part of the problem-solving procedure.

Eating Behavior Review. The same procedure should now be used for eating behaviors, with the group using the Activity Checklist as the basis for filling in the problem-solving list and then using group discussion and input to help with problem solving. The therapist should stress the steps needed to adequately solve a problem: identifying the problem, devising an intervention, and implementing an intervention. If the problem is not solved, the process should begin again.

Food Choices. The same process should be repeated for food choices, emphasizing the need to reduce fat and animal protein and alcohol intake, and substitute complex carbohydrates. Again, it should be suggested that those with problems should begin to keep food records for a few weeks to help identify and change further problems.

Environmental Influences and Cognitive Ecology. Exactly the same process should be used to solve problems in the area of environmental influences and cognitive distortions.

As previously noted, each session should follow the same basic outline, although the content and focus of each session will vary, depending upon the problems identified by group members. As is the case in teaching other sessions of the course, individuals who are not showing adequate progress should be scheduled for an individual assessment to determine if additional approaches to their problem might be necessary.

PHARMACOLOGIC APPROACHES TO STRENGTHENING WEIGHT LOSS

There is no doubt that anorectic agents such as fenfluramine hydrochloride (Pondimin®) lead to enhanced weight loss when combined with a behavioral approach over the short term. Unfortunately, such an advantage does not appear to be well maintained, and the final place of pharmacologic agents in weight control is not yet entirely clear.

Fenfluramine has a structure similar to amphetamine. Unlike the latter compound, however, it does not appear to be addictive, nor does it have the activating properties of psychostimulants. The side effects of fenfluramine are relatively few. Some persons experience sedation, which almost always clears in a few days. More rarely an activating effect is experienced, and an occasional patient will not be able to tolerate the medication because of the extent of the activation. Another relatively rare side effect is diarrhoea, which again may be severe enough to warrant stopping the medication. Persons with a history of depression should be treated cautiously with the medication because it has been observed that sudden cessation of fenfluramine may precipitate depression. The usual dosage given to patients is 120 mg per day in divided doses—usually 3 times daily about 30 minutes before eating. Some individuals may need less medication, or a different dosage schedule, depending upon the exact nature of their eating disorder. It is useful, therefore, to build up the dosage gradually over a week or 2.

Several studies investigating the combination of fenfluramine and behavior therapy in the management of the obese patient have been reported during the past few years. In the most comprehensive study of this issue (Craighead, Stunkard, & O'Brien, 1981), obese patients were allocated at random to one of four groups: fenfluramine administered in a physician's office, group-conducted behavior therapy, fenfluramine plus nondirective group therapy, and a combination of drug and behavior therapy. The least effective condition was fenfluramine administered in a physician's office with a weight loss of 6.4 kg after 6 months of treatment. Adding group support enhanced the efficacy of fenfluramine therapy, with patients losing 14.0 kg, presumably due to enhanced compliance with the drug regimen. Behavioral treatment led to weight losses averaging 10.9 kg, whereas the combination of drug and behavioral treatment led to a mean weight loss of 14.5 kg.

At 1-year follow-up this picture had changed. Those receiving behavior therapy alone showed the least tendency to regain weight. These patients had lost significantly more weight at follow-up than those in the combined treatment condition. Participants who received fenfluramine without behavior therapy fared the worst. This finding underscores the usefulness of behavior-change procedures in promoting maintenance of weight losses.

Another study, however, began to point the way toward a potential use for fenfluramine. In this study the effect of different sequences of behavior therapy and medication were compared (Craighead, 1984). At 1-year follow-up those receiving the delayed introduction of drug tended to lose more weight than those receiving early introduction of the medication. In particular, those who lost little weight with behavior therapy showed substantial improvement when treated with fenfluramine. These poor responders may be an excellent subgroup for the delayed introduction of this drug.

A further potential application of fenfluramine may be for the obese binge eater. As noted in chapter 3, such individuals respond less well to behavior therapy, losing only half as much weight as the nonbinge eater (Keefe at al., 1984). Recent work suggests that the carbohydrate craving often associated with binge eating may be modifiable using fenfluramine in smaller than usual dosage (Wurtman et al., 1985). In this study, obese inpatients were given either 15 mg of fenfluramine or its placebo twice daily for two periods of 8 days each. These patients could obtain snacks freely from a vending machine on the ward. Under these conditions, fenfluramine was found to reduce the consumption of simple carbohydrates at meals by 22% with no effect upon protein intake. In addition, consumption of simple carbohydrates during snacks was reduced by 41%, with a significant reduction in overall caloric intake.

From a clinical viewpoint, it may be worthwhile to place patients who do not lose weight in the first few sessions of behavior therapy on fenfluramine. In the behavior therapy program described in the previous chapter this would take place following the evaluation of progress in Session 5. For the obese binge eater, small doses of medication should be used—usually 20 mg twice daily taken in the midafternoon and during the evening, the times at which carbohydrate cravings are usually at their peak. For the obese nonbinge eater, high-dose fenfluramine therapy should be used. In both cases such therapy might be continued for a longer than usual duration, perhaps for as long as 6 months or 1 year, before a trial discontinuation is considered. Meanwhile, patients should be taught the full range of behavior-change procedures in an effort to combat relapse when the medication is withdrawn.

A recent controlled study suggests that a different pharmacologic approach, antidepressant treatment, may be useful in the treatment of obesity when combined with a behavioral approach to weight reduction (Nutzinger, Cayiroglu, Sachs, & Zapotoczky, 1985). In this study, mildly depressed women receiving behavioral treatment for obesity were randomly allocated after 4 weeks of treatment to receive either doxepin hydrochloride (an antidepressant) or its placebo. This tested the hypothesis that weight reduction increases depressive symptoms, and that this increase would be relieved by antidepressant treatment, with a beneficial effect upon weight loss.

During the first 4 weeks of treatment, patients in the behavioral weight-loss program evidenced an increase in depressive symptoms. After randomization to doxepin or to its placebo, these depressive symptoms showed greater improvement for those receiving the antidepressant, but these differences were not statistically significant at any point during the 1-year follow-up. On the other hand, those receiving the placebo showed an increase in weight at the 6-month follow-up, which persisted during the remainder of the study, whereas those receiving the antidepressant showed a continued weight loss (7.3 kg vs. 3.0 kg at 1-year follow-up).

These findings must be regarded as preliminary at present. Nonetheless, this study suggests that mildly depressed overweight clients might maintain their weight losses better if treated with an antidepressant medication in addition to receiving behavioral treatment.

VERY-LOW-CALORIE DIETS

Another approach to enhancing initial weight loss in the obese patient is the use of a very-low-calorie diet under careful medical supervision. At present, the research literature concerning the long-term results of such therapy is meager. Nonetheless, it is clear that substantial weight is lost by using such diets, a larger weight loss than that achievable by means of behavior therapy alone, although this beneficial effect may be offset in part by higher drop-out rates.

The very-low-calorie diet is usually defined as one containing less than 500 calories/day, and is obtainable in both liquid and solid versions. Unfortunately, an unusual number of deaths were reported for obese individuals using a very-low-calorie diet containing poor quality protein (Linn and Stuart, 1976). The mechanism responsible for these deaths appeared to be protein depletion combined with potassium deficiency (Frank, Graham, & Frank, 1981). This combination appears to cause fatal ventricular arrhythmias in some patients (Isner, Sours, Paris, Farrans, & Roberts, 1979). On the other hand, very-low-calorie diets containing high-quality protein and administered under medical supervision do not appear to be associated with a higher than expected death rate among users.

The efficacy of these diets in the short term is now quite clear. There is a linear relationship between weight loss and the length of time that individuals remain on the diet. After 12 weeks of dieting, the average weight loss is greater than 20 kg. Many patients tolerate the diet well and do not experience undue hunger while remaining on the diet. Unfortunately, the drop-out rate varies between 30 and 50% in uncontrolled studies, far higher than that experienced with behavioral procedures alone. In addition, maintenance of weight loss may be problematic because most studies suggest that weight gradually returns towards pre-diet levels.

The only controlled study addressing these issues was recently completed (Wadden & Stunkard, 1986). Subjects were randomly allocated to either the very-low-calorie diet or behavior therapy alone, or a combination of the two treatments. At the end of 4-months treatment, those in the combined treatment group had lost 19.3 kg as compared with 14.0 kg for the other two groups. At 1-year follow-up, all groups had regained some weight. The combined-treatment group had now lost 12.9 kg, the behavior-therapy-alone group, 9.5 kg, and the very-low-calorie diet group, 4.6 kg. Such relapse may, of course, be remediable by using more careful shaping procedures as the diet is stopped and the consumption of food is begun again. Undoubtedly, research over the next few years will clarify these issues.

At present, the indications for advising the use of a very-low-calorie diet in conjunction with behavior therapy would appear to be as follows:

1. If an adequate trial of behavior therapy for obesity fails to achieve satisfactory weight loss;
2. For individuals who are more than 50 lbs overweight;
3. For individuals whose obesity poses a greater than usual health risk;
4. In the case of the massively obese, where surgery (gastroplasty) may be needed because of the health risks involved, a trial of very-low-calorie diet may be appropriate in an effort to avoid surgery;
5. For individuals who have had gastroplasty and who are beginning to regain weight.

A Very-Low-Calorie Diet Program

Because medical, nutritional, and behavioral complications can occur with the use of a very-low-calorie diet, it is essential that such diets are conducted within a specialized multidisciplinary program that can provide medical supervision, nutritional advice, and a behavioral approach to weight control. The major medical contraindications to participation are recent myocardial infarction, a history of stroke, poorly controlled diabetes mellitus, and active peptic ulcer. Psychiatric contraindications include current severe depression or a history of major suicidal attempts, or the current use of lithium carbonate, phenothiazines, or tricyclic antidepressants, because these agents predispose to cardiac arrhythmias and stable blood levels of the medication may be more difficult to maintain on a very-low-calorie diet. Pregnancy is an absolute contraindication for the use of such diets.

Before being admitted to the program, potential patients must undergo a comprehensive physical examination, together with an electrocardiogram, and assays of blood chemistry focusing on electrolytes, liver, and kidney function. The psychological assessment described earlier for behavior-change programs should also be carried out.

The very-low-calorie diet is usually prescribed for a 12-week period, although longer intervals have been used. The patient then enters a maintenance phase, with a return to normal meals, and may subsequently begin another diet cycle. Group meetings should be held in conjunction with the diet, being at first supportive and educational about the diet and its use, and then moving toward behavioral management. A behavioral weight-loss program such as the one described earlier in this book, with some modification of timing, is a necessary supplement to the very-low-calorie diet.

These behavior-change sessions should be continued through the reintroduction of solid food, with emphasis upon eating style, exercise, and dietary content, followed by a maintenance program similar to that described earlier in this chapter. The lack of research in the area of very-low-calorie diets has led to a lack of knowledge regarding the selection of particular procedures for the reintroduction of solid food. Should, for example, solid food be introduced gradually or all at once? Should a modified diet be used for some time, for example, one or two solid meals supplemented by a very-low-calorie diet? Unfortunately, no satisfactory answer to these important questions is available, although it would seem on general principle that a slow reintroduction of solid food would be the preferred method.

COMPUTERIZED WEIGHT-LOSS PROGRAMS

The procedural specification of the behavioral approach to the treatment of overweightness makes it ideal for translation to the computer. As we have seen, behavior therapy programs include the provision of information, therapeutic instructions, self-monitoring, feedback, and reinforcement, with the aim of altering eating style, increasing activity levels, and reducing caloric intake. The precise contribution of these processes and procedures to weight loss is not entirely clear at present. Some studies demonstrate clear relationships between some procedures and weight loss, and other studies find no such relationship (Brownell and Stunkard, 1978; Johnson, Wildman, & O'Brien, 1980; Lansky, 1978). Methodologic problems, including the error of measurement due to reliance on self-report, and small sample size probably account for some of the negative results in this area.

Recently, however, a prospective study found that many of the behavior changes hypothesized to be crucial to weight reduction were, in fact, significantly correlated with weight loss (Stalonas & Kirschenbaum, 1985). These included self-monitoring, exercise, and eating-behavior changes. It therefore seems likely that specific behavior changes are related to weight loss, and that processes such as feedback and reinforcement that have been demonstrated to be successful in other behavior therapies are also crucial to effecting the necessary behavior changes. These processes and procedures can then form the basis for a computerized approach to weight reduction.

Potential advantages for computerized versions of weight-management programs include ease of access to the program, which is independent of therapist time; treatment in the client's own environment; and enhanced cost-effectiveness. Calculations based upon the current cost of therapist-conducted programs suggest that the cost of computer-based therapy would be between one third and one sixth of the usual behavioral treatment.

The development of small lightweight portable computers allows for a convenient sophisticated application of behavior therapy with minimal interaction with a therapist. A recent small-scale controlled test of the effectiveness of such a computer with obese individuals provided encouraging results (Burnett, Taylor, & Agras, 1985). Twelve subjects matched on BMI were allocated at random to either computer therapy or to a control condition using 'paper-and-pencil methods for goal setting, self-monitoring, and feedback, and matched as to therapist contact time. Weight loss for the 8 post-baseline weeks was 3.7 kg for computer-treated subjects and 1.5 kg for control subjects ($p < .05$). Because a reversal design was also used in this experiment, the subjects received only 6 weeks of therapy in both groups. These results suggest that computer therapy is likely to be reasonably successful in producing weight loss. At 8-months follow-up, the computer-treated subjects had now lost 8.0 kg as compared with 1.0 kg for the controls, even though the computer had not been used during the follow-up period. This suggests that maintenance of weight loss may be very good with computer therapy.

A Computer Program for Weight Loss

An advanced version of the computer program used in the above experiment is now commercially available. This program, CADET II (Computer-assisted Diet and Exercise Training Program), uses a small hand-held computer measuring 8" × 3.5" × 1" with a two-line liquid crystal display featuring both text and graphic feedback. The main features of the program, each of which are accessed through a menu, are described in the following paragraphs.

Goal Setting. Participants are advised not to set goals for a few days so that they can gain an idea of their usual caloric intake and activity levels. After that time, the program prompts the user to set a daily caloric limit for meals and for snacks, slowly reducing from present levels and not lower than 1,200 calories per day. Activity goals are similarly set using an energy-use point system dependent upon the vigor of the activity engaged in.

Self-Monitoring. This aspect of the program prompts for type of report, for example, meal, snack, or exercise, and for information within each of these categories. For food reports, the program asks for the first meal item, to which the user responds by typing in the number of calories for the first food item eaten in a meal or snack, using the calorie guide. A second prompt asks for portion size. The program continues to prompt for subsequent food items until the return key is pressed without entering a value, returning the user to the main menu.

Planning. The entry system can also be used in the planning mode, in which case the items typed will not be stored in memory. In this way the user can plan meals or activities and consider the effect on the day's goal.

Feedback. Calories consumed (noted separately for meals and snacks, as well as totalled) or activity engaged in can be summarized at any time during the 24-hour period. Both cumulative absolute values and the percentage of goal attainment are displayed. Positive evaluative statements are automatically provided in this mode.

Timer Function. This function is used to help slow down the rate of eating during meals. The user selects the duration of time for the meal, and the computer displays a countdown, as well as occasional advice to the user.

Cognitive Change. Although a computer cannot challenge verbal expressions of beliefs and attitudes, it can prompt more adaptive cognitions. In the "Slim thoughts" sequence, the user can either rely on a list of prompts selected by the computer or type in personalized cognitive reminders to be displayed in this mode.

Graphic Feedback. A 14-day plot of caloric intake and activity levels that is continually automatically updated is provided in this mode. In addition, the user can enter daily weight, which is transformed to a graphic display. In this way longer-term progress can be reviewed by the user and the relationships between caloric intake, activity, and weight easily observed.

Information regarding this computer system, which is available together with an illustrated instruction manual, a motivational tape, and a calorie guide, is obtainable from Behavioral Science Products Inc., 451 Chaucer Street, Palo Alto, California 94301-2202.

Chapter 5
The Treatment of Bulimia

Bulimia, as we saw in chapter 1, appears to have rapidly increased in prevalence during the late 1970s, due in part to the increasing social pressure upon women to achieve a thin body shape and the use of dietary methods to achieve this end. Because only a small fraction of young women respond to such societal pressures by developing bulimia, we must assume that a predisposition to develop the disorder exists, a predisposition that might be either biological or psychological in nature. Among the potential predisposing factors is an excessive prevalence of severe depression in the first-degree relatives of bulimics, suggesting a possible genetic linkage between depression and bulimia. From this, perspective bulimia can be viewed as a variant of affective disorder.

It is widely agreed that dieting leads to a tendency to binge on sweet foods, and that in turn, binge eating leads to weight gain and hence to purging in an attempt to reinstate control over weight and body shape. Both biologic and psychologic factors may play a part in this sequence of events, as discussed in chapter 1.

These observations concerning the development of bulimia have led to two approaches to treatment. The first, psychological, aims at interrupting the restricted eating pattern using cognitive-behavioral therapy. The second, pharmacological, aims at relieving the depression hypothesized to underlie the disorder, using antidepressant medication. Both controlled and uncontrolled studies in each of these areas have not been reported, so that a beginning foundation for the treatment of bulimia has been laid.

COGNITIVE-BEHAVIORAL THERAPY—THE RESEARCH BACKGROUND

The cognitive-behavioral approach to the treatment of bulimia derives from three sources: descriptive studies illuminating the pathogenic process of bulimia, social learning theory upon which the therapeutic principles are based

61

(Bandura, 1977), and developments in cognitive–behavioral approaches to conditions such as depression, from which some of the specific procedures derive (Beck, 1976).

The main therapeutic procedures used in cognitive behavioral therapy, as first described by Fairburn (1981), are aimed at interrupting the revolving cycle of dietary restriction, binge eating, and purging by reinstating normal dietary habits while challenging the distorted beliefs that accompany the disorder. In brief, the first step is to enhance social control by urging the patient to disclose the full nature of the problem to significant others. Following this, the restricted dietary pattern, which is identified through the use of self-monitoring, is tackled by gradually shaping the client's eating behavior toward a balanced diet of three meals a day. Exposure to binge foods is then accomplished by introducing small amounts of such foods into the diet. This process is usually made problematic by the client's distorted cognitions concerning food and body image. Such cognitions are identified and modified by challenge and the application of logic, thus clearing the way for the patient to try out the necessary behavior changes. In the final phase of therapy, procedures to reduce the chance of relapse are used, including reestablishing self-monitoring, problem solving, coping with high-risk situations, and obtaining help from friends.

According to Fairburn (1981), vomiting should diminish steadily as the eating behavior becomes less restrictive, and little specific attention to the symptom of vomiting is needed other than engaging in distracting activities when the urge is felt. Others, however, have suggested that the addition of exposure to binge foods under therapist supervision, with attendant prevention of vomiting, may be helpful. Such procedures are derived from the treatment of phobias and compulsive behavior, in which they have shown much utility (Leitenberg, Agras, Edwards, & Thompson, 1970; Mills, Agras, Barlow, Baugh, & Mills, 1973). As we have seen, bulimia can be regarded as a phobia of becoming fat. As a consequence, foods defined as "fattening" are assiduously avoided. Vomiting can be viewed as anxiety-reducing behavior, relieving the fear of becoming fat in much the same way that compulsive behavior reduces phobic anxiety. Thus, exposure to the feared foods, combined with prevention of vomiting (response prevention of vomiting under therapist supervision), is a logical extension of treatment.

The first series of cases treated with a cognitive behavioral approach was reported by Fairburn (1981). He treated 11 patients individually for an average of 7 months, beginning with two to three sessions each week followed by weekly, and then biweekly sessions. Nine of the 11 patients reduced their binge eating and vomiting to less than once per month, and this improvement was maintained in the 9 patients for whom follow-up data were available. Fairburn reports that the participants in this study showed no significant weight gains. A group adaptation of Fairburn's method also appeared successful in an uncontrolled study, with self-induced vomiting dropping from 24 episodes per week to 2.2 times per week by the end of 16 weeks of treatment (Schneider & Agras,

1985). A 6-month follow-up demonstrated some relapse, with vomiting averaging 3.8 per week. However, follow-up at 30 months showed no further relapse, with vomiting averaging 1.6 per week (a reduction of 93%).

The first controlled treatment study reported in 1983 used a modification of cognitive–behavioral therapy combined with "insight" therapy that was compared with a waiting-list control group (Lacey, 1983). Patients received a 30-minute individual session, focusing upon "simple behavioral and counseling techniques before moving on to insight directed psychotherapy." Following the individual session, patients met together in small groups for 90 minutes. The treatment program lasted for 10 weeks. A major focus of the program was on self-monitoring of eating behavior and the formulation of a weekly contract to change eating behavior by reducing binge eating and vomiting and consuming more normal meals.

No improvement was noted in those in the waiting-list control group. For those receiving treatment, there was a 96% reduction in binge eating and purging by the end of 10 weeks, and 24 of 30 patients had stopped binge eating and vomiting completely by the end of treatment. There was little evidence of relapse during the 2-year follow-up. No patients dropped out during the initial period of treatment, and only 7% had dropped out during follow-up. In contrast to other studies, depression scores increased during the course of treatment, despite the successful reductions in bulimic symptoms.

A second treatment/no treatment comparison was recently published (Wolchik, Weiss, & Katzman, 1986). Thirteen women with bulimia received treatment and seven women were in the no-treatment control group. It should be noted that allocation to the experimental conditions was nonrandom. The group treatment consisted of a "psychoeducational" approach, which included the following elements: self-disclosure in the group aimed at reducing guilt, self-monitoring, nutritional information, alternatives to binge eating, investigation of affective responses, assertiveness, and the implications of cultural expectations regarding body shape and body image exercises. Seven sessions were given.

Two women dropped out of treatment, so the analyses were conducted on the 11 survivors. The treatment group showed a significantly greater reduction in binge eating, purging, and depression, as well as a significantly superior increase in self-esteem. Reductions in purging were 52.7% at immediate outcome, and 60.6% at 10 weeks post-treatment. Only one third of the women ceased purging. The results of this treatment do not appear to be as good as those described in the study conducted by Lacey (1983), although we do not know whether this was due to differences in the therapeutic procedures used, or to the lesser duration of treatment, or even to population differences between the two studies.

Another study provided the third comparison of treatment with no treatment (Lee & Rush, 1986). Thirty subjects meeting *DSM-III* criteria for bulimia were allocated at random to either a waiting-list condition or to 12 sessions of treatment over a 6-week period. Treatment was focused first upon relaxation train-ing as an alternative to binge eating, and second upon identifying and challenging dysfunctional cognitions. Altering the frequency and content of meals was less stressed than in the usual cognitive–behavioral treatment. The waiting-list control group showed no improvement in terms of binge eating or vomiting, whereas the treatment group reduced their binge eating and vomiting by about 70%. It should be noted, however, that only 27% of subjects ceased to binge eat and purge by the end of the study. The authors suggest that an extended treatment might have strengthened the therapeutic efficacy of this treatment package.

Although these three studies are encouraging, we cannot conclude that the specific therapeutic procedures used were responsible for improvement, because of the absence of an active control condition. This question was addressed in a study of group-conducted cognitive–behavioral treatment (Kirkley, Schneider, Agras, & Bachman, 1985). Twenty-eight women between the ages of 18 and 46 years, and with an average age of 28 years, were randomly allocated either to the full cognitive behavioral group-treatment package or to a control condition. The latter consisted of weekly group meetings for a 16-week period, self-disclo-sure of the problem behavior in the group context, self-monitoring of eating behavior, including binge eating and vomiting, and discussion of such behavior and its implications for the patients. No specific behavioral advice was given to these participants. Those in the cognitive–behavioral group received the full treatment package following the description provided by Fairburn (1981) and the procedures used in the uncontrolled study of group-conducted cognitive–behavioral therapy (Schneider & Agras, 1985). Both treatment groups were led by a pair of PhD clinical psychologists.

The cognitive–behavioral treatment had fewer drop-outs than the control condition (8% vs. 36%), and these drop-outs tended to be younger, to have had their bulimia for a shorter time, and to show higher scores on the Beck Depres-sion Inventory. This finding suggests that the greater structure associated with cognitive–behavioral therapy may help the younger patient to stay in therapy. Those receiving cognitive–behavioral treatment showed a 95% reduction in binge eating and vomiting during the 16 weeks of treatment, significantly greater than the reduction in the control group. Again, there was evidence of some relapse at follow-up, suggesting the need to improve relapse-prevention strategies. Measures of psychological functioning, including depression, showed equal improvement in both groups during the course of treatment. Degree of initial depression did not predict treatment outcome. Because mea-sures of therapy credibility were equal between the two groups, we can conclude that the behavioral procedures used were responsible for the differential treat-ment outcome between them. It should also be noted that group support, self-monitoring, and disclosure of the problem led to sizeable reductions in binge eating and purging.

An analysis of the food records of subjects completing treatment in this study suggests that restricted eating habits may persist despite an apparently successful treatment outcome (Kirkley, Agras, & Weiss, 1985). As has been reported previously, the caloric intake of subjects prior to treatment was very high, averaging nearly 4,500 Kcal/day, and ranging from 450 to 18,202 Kcal/day. Following treatment, those patients who had ceased to purge had an average daily intake of 1,458 Kcal. Many of these participants had signficant inadequacies in their diets at this time, the basis for suspecting that dietary restriction persisted.

Response-Prevention Treatment

The utility of response prevention of vomiting has also been studied in both uncontrolled and controlled studies. Apart from case reports involving a single subject, the first uncontrolled study of a series of cases using response prevention was reported in 1984. Five bulimic women were treated with this method, in which they ate binge food and then remained with the therapist until the urge to vomit had dissipated (Leitenberg, Gross, Peterson, & Rosen, 1984). Cognitions provoked by the binge eating were examined and challenged. Self-reported anxiety levels declined during the response-prevention session, and also across sessions. One of the five subjects showed no improvement despite additional treatment; the other subjects showed a satisfactory decline in binge eating and vomiting.

In the largest uncontrolled study of the use of response prevention to date, the results of treatment of 34 bulimic women in a private practice were reported (Giles, Young, & Young, 1985). Eighteen percent of these women dropped out of treatment, a proportion larger than those reported in studies of cognitive-behavioral treatment. The more anxiety-provoking treatment may therefore be associated with a higher drop-out rate. It should be noted, parenthetically, that considerable resistance to response prevention may occur, with patients "forgetting" to bring binge food to the session, missing sessions, and so on. A very supportive relationship is needed in order to work out these problems engendered by the anxiety-provoking aspects of this procedure. Sixty-two percent of the patients showed greater than an 80% reduction in binge eating and vomiting during treatment that averaged 12 weeks in duration. Eighteen percent of the patients did not respond to treatment.

A recent study compared the combination of cognitive–behavioral treatment and response prevention to a waiting-list control condition (Ordman & Kirschenbaum, 1985). Twenty bulimic women meeting DSM-III criteria for bulimia were allocated at random to either treatment (averaging 15 sessions) or to a waiting list. The full range of therapeutic procedures was used in this study, although not all the women monitored their meal frequency and food intake. Those in the waiting-list condition reduced their vomiting frequency by 33% as compared to 84% in the active-treatment condition, a statistically significant difference. However, only 20% of the treatment group stopped binge eating and purging by the end of treatment.

In another controlled study, a cognitive treatment of bulimia was compared with cognitive treatment plus response prevention of vomiting (Wilson, Rossiter, Kleifield, & Lindholm, 1986). It should be noted that the cognitive restructuring method used here differs considerably from the cognitive–behavioral treatment described in previous studies, because it focused almost exclusively upon cognitions, with less emphasis upon normalizing eating, adding small amounts of binge food to the diet, and so on. In response prevention, beginning in Session 5, subjects brought in binge food to the treatment sessions and were asked to eat enough to bring about the urge to induce vomiting.

Twenty-four percent of the 17 subjects involved in this study dropped out before the conclusion of treatment, with the drop-outs equally divided between the two treatment conditions. Those in the response-prevention condition lowered their self-induced vomiting by 94%, a statistically significant decrease, whereas those in the cognitive–behavioral condition reduced their vomiting by 71%, a decrease that was not significant. It should be noted, however, that those receiving cognitive–behavioral treatment alone did not reduce their vomiting as much as participants in the other studies of cognitive–behavioral treatment previously described, where decreases in excess of 90% were the rule. This may have been due to the focus on cognitions, rather than on behavior change, in this condition. The major contribution of response prevention appears to have been in strengthening the maintenance of treatment effects, because only one of the seven patients receiving response prevention had relapsed 1 year after treatment. From this study we can conclude that response prevention of vomiting exerts a specific effect in the treatment of bulimia.

The results of both uncontrolled and controlled studies are quite consistent. Cognitive–behavioral treatment, with or without response prevention, results in impressive reductions in binge eating and vomiting, and concomitant improvement in psychological functioning. Cognitive–behavioral treatment has been demonstrated to be superior to an active control condition that did not include the specific behavioral procedures. Similarly, the specific effects of the procedures of response prevention have been delineated. This finding suggests that support groups without the use of specific behavioral procedures may not be the ideal way to treat bulimia. The addition of response prevention to the cognitive–behavioral package may prove useful in increasing the number of patients who are abstinent by the end of treatment, and also in reducing the relapse rate, which has been noted to be a problem in controlled studies of cognitive–behavioral treatment.

We may conclude that there is a narrow, but promising research basis for the use of cognitive–behavioral therapy as originally described by Fairburn (1981), and that initial evidence suggests that response prevention of vomiting should be added to this basic package. It is reasonable to caution the reader at this point that the research literature in this area is evolving rapidly, and that these conclusions, particularly the role of response prevention in treatment, may have to be modified in the light of new evidence.

PHARMACOLOGIC THERAPY— THE RESEARCH BACKGROUND

As noted earlier in this chapter, the pharmacologic approach to the treatment of bulimia is based on the hypothesis that bulimia is a form of affective disorder, or that alternatively, antidepressants, as they do in anxiety disorder, reduce anxiety (and depression) and hence the tendency to binge and purge. Both uncontrolled and controlled studies of the use of antidepressant medication in bulimic patients have been reported.

Several series of patients treated with one or another of the antidepressants have been reported (Jonas, Hudson, & Pope, 1983; Pope & Hudson, 1982; Stewart, Walsh, Wright, Roose, & Glassman, 1984). Some 75% of bulimic patients treated with either imipramine or monoamine oxidase inhibitors show improvement in terms of reduction in binge eating. Withdrawal of medication, however, was almost always accompanied by a relapse, and other patients relapse despite being continued on medication. A somewhat more pessimistic account of the use of antidepressant agents in the depressed bulimic suggested that a much lower proportion of bulimics respond well (a 50% or greater reduction in binge eating, which was maintained) to this treatment (Brotman, Herzog, & Woods, 1984). Only 7 of 22 subjects (32%) met this criterion for improvement because 5 initial responders relapsed while still on medication.

One problem with the pharmacologic treatment of bulimics is that medication may be vomited along with food. Hence, Pope and his co-workers emphasize the need to monitor blood levels of medication during treatment to ensure that an adequate dose is being achieved. A further problem arises with monoamine oxidase inhibitors; namely, that certain dietary restrictions have to be followed. Patients with bulimia may have difficulty in adhering to such restrictions because they perceive their eating to be out of control. Nonetheless, the initial uncontrolled research in this area is encouraging.

The first controlled outcome study, comparing imipramine with a placebo in a double blind design, was reported in 1983 (Pope, Hudson, Jonas, & Yurgelun-Todd, 1983). Twenty-two patients meeting *DSM-III* criteria for bulimia were randomly allocated to either the placebo or imipramine. Patients who had previously been treated with antidepressant medication or with electroshock therapy, or who had significant suicidal ideation, were excluded from this study. At the end of this 6-week trial, two patients had dropped out of the imipramine group and one from the placebo group. Patients who had received imipramine showed a decline in self-reported binge eating of 70%, whereas those in the placebo group showed virtually no change, a statistically significant difference between the two groups. In addition, scores on the Hamilton Depression Scale were significantly lower in those receiving imipramine. There was also a correlation between change in the Hamilton scores and improvement in binge eating ($r =$ 0.65). This correlation was interpreted to mean that there was a relationship between the antidepressant effect of imipramine and improvement in binge eating. However, it should be noted that the correlation could as easily imply that improvement in binge eating leads to improvement in depression, as appears to be the case in cognitive–behavioral therapy.

In a second double-blind controlled trial of antidepressant therapy, the monoamine oxidase inhibitor phenelzine sulfate was compared with a placebo (Walsh, Stewart, Roose, Gladis, & Glassman, 1984). Twenty women meeting the DSM-III criteria for bulimia, and binge eating at least 3 times weekly, were entered into the study, with 9 receiving active medication and 11 the placebo. Thirty-five women had qualified for the study, and 15 of these had been excluded in a placebo washout phase, either because they improved or because they were unable to keep appointments or adhere to the study medication and dietary requirements. Of those entered into the study, only 15 completed the 8-week trial. Thus, the number of patients deemed suitable for the medication trial, or who were able to comply with the requirements of the trial, was very large. (Excluding the placebo responders, only 47% of subjects were able to complete the study.)

Those receiving active medication reduced their binge eating by 76%, whereas those in the placebo group reduced by just 5%, a significant difference between the groups. The authors note that patients who showed no signs of depression responded as well as those who were depressed or who had a past history of major depression. They concluded that phenelzine might be reducing the persistent dysphoria (a state of anxiety or tension that precedes binge eating) commonly experienced by bulimic individuals, rather than reducing depression.

A trial of amitriptyline in bulimic patients reported a somewhat different pattern of results to the previous two studies, perhaps because self-monitoring and a prescription to eat regularly, described as a minimal behavioral program, was used in both the drug and placebo groups (Mitchell & Groat, 1984). Those receiving medication reduced their binge eating by 72.1%, a level comparable to the studies previously noted, but those in the placebo group reduced their binge eating by 51.9%. Thus, there was no significant difference between the groups on any measure of bulimia, although there was a significant difference in favor of those receiving imipramine in ratings on the Hamilton Depression Scale posttreatment. Depressed individuals showed considerably less improvement in their bulimic symptoms than those who were not depressed. Presumably, the use of simple behavioral procedures in this study augmented the therapeutic response of those receiving the placebo, a result somewhat comparable to the effect of self-monitoring and group support in the Kirkley et al. (1985) study of group-conducted cognitive–behavioral therapy.

A study in our own clinic again provided some evidence for the efficacy of imipramine in the treatment of bulimia. This study extended over 16 weeks and is the pharmacologic study of longest duration reported to date (Agras, Dorian, Kirkley, Arnow, & Bachman, in press). Twenty-two bulimic women participated in this double-blind placebo-controlled trial in which the patients saw a psychiatrist for brief medication visits during which they received no behavioral advice. Two patients, both in the placebo group, dropped out of this study because of side effects to the medication. By the 16th week of treatment, those receiving the active medication had reduced their self-induced vomiting by 79%, whereas those in the placebo group showed reductions of 43%. This difference was statistically significant. However, only 30% of the patients in the imipramine group were free of vomiting by the end of the study. No relationship was found between baseline depression scores on the Beck Inventory and improvement in bulimic conditions.

In another study, desipramine appeared to have excellent antibulimic properties, perhaps better than imipramine in this regard (Hughes, Wells, Cunningham, & Ilstrup, 1986). Twenty-five participants meeting *DSM-III* criteria for bulimia and without evidence of major depression were randomly allocated to receive either desipramine or a placebo. Those receiving the placebo were offered the active drug after 6 weeks of therapy. The target dose of the medication was 200 mg, although this was adjusted, depending upon blood levels and side effects. Three of the 13 patients (23%) allocated to the active drug dropped out of the study because of side effects. Binge eating was reduced by 91% in those receiving active medication, whereas this symptom increased by 19% in the control group. No comparable data were given for purging frequency, although the authors note that 15 patients became abstinent, an abstinence rate of 60%, approximately double that observed in other drug studies. At 10-weeks follow-up, the improvements noted at 6 weeks were not only maintained, but had in some cases been extended.

Overall, then, there is evidence that antidepressant agents produce improvement in binge eating and self-induced vomiting, at least in the short term, although for most studies the improvement is not as great as that for cognitive–behavioral therapy. Maintenance of improvement, both while still on the medication and after stopping the medication, is a problem. With the exception of desipramine, a relatively small proportion of patients stop binge eating and vomiting. The evidence that the more depressed patient does better with antidepressant therapy than the nondepressed patient is not great; in fact, some studies have reported that the depressed patient does less well. In the only study to examine this issue, no relationship was found between baseline depression scores and outcome in terms of reduction in bulimic symptoms.

DRUG TREATMENT OF BULIMIA

What then is the place of antidepressant treatment in bulimia? One possibility, given the relatively low cost of medication therapy as compared with cognitive–behavioral therapy, is that a trial of such medication should be the first step in the treatment of bulimics, provided that patients do not meet any of the exclusion criteria for medication. Such exclusions include pregnancy (or the use of inadequate birth-control methods), current suicidal urges (too great a risk of attempting suicide while on the medication), and of course, previous adequate trials of medication without a therapeutic response. In the case of the monoamine oxidase inhibitors, the ability to comply with dietary restrictions should be carefully assessed, perhaps using a trial period of self-monitoring after being given the dietary instruction and before starting medication. Among the foods to be avoided are those containing a high concentration of tyramine or dopamine, including high protein foods that have undergone aging or fermentation, pickling, smoking, or bacterial contamination; cheeses; pickled herring; beer; wine; liver; yeast extract (including brewers yeast); dry sausage (including salami, pepperoni, and bologna); pods of broad beans; and yogurt. In addition, sympathomimetic agents such as amphetamines, or cocaine, should not be taken in conjunction with monoamine oxidase inhibitors. All these substances may cause rapid and excessive rises in blood pressure that may be life-threatening.

It should also be noted that quite a significant number of bulimic individuals are not willing to take medication. Walsh et al. (1984) found that one quarter of their potential subjects were either unwilling or uninterested in taking medication. Such patients should be referred for cognitive–behavioral treatment.

Assessment should follow that described in chapter 2 for the bulimic individual. Because self-monitoring appears to have a significant effect upon binge eating and vomiting, it would seem worthwhile for the physician to ask patients to self-monitor their binge eating, vomiting, and laxative use during the course of medication taking. Dosage levels reported in the literature appear to be similar to those used in the treatment of major depression. Imipramine and desipramine would seem to be the drugs of choice, given the problems of using monoamine oxidase inhibitors in this group of patients. Because some patients develop marked side effects with low doses of imipramine, treatment should begin with 25 mg of imipramine taken at night, and should be increased, depending upon the tolerance of side effects and the response in terms of binge eating and vomiting. The time course of action of the medication appears to be similar to that for the treatment of depression, with improvement occurring after the third week of treatment. As previously noted, blood levels of imipramine or desipramine should be obtained after a stable dosage level is reached.

Because only one third to two thirds of patients treated with antidepressants are likely to cease binge eating and vomiting entirely, many patients will require further treatment. Thus cognitive–behavioral therapy, as described in the next chapter, should follow medication treatment when the patient is unable to entirely stop binge eating and vomiting. Unfortunately, no study has compared cognitive–behavioral therapy with and without medication, thus the additive effects of medication to cognitive–behavioral therapy are unknown at this point.

Similarly, very little is known regarding the fate of patients once the medication regimen is discontinued. There is, however, a strong impression in the literature that many patients relapse quickly. Our experience has also been that relapse is frequent, even following treatment for up to 18 months, suggesting that patients do not learn more adaptive behavior patterns during this time. At present, a trial of medication discontinuation should be made at six monthly intervals. Should relapse continue to be a problem, the addition of cognitive–behavioral treatment to gradual drug withdrawal should be tried.

Chapter 6

A Cognitive–Behavioral
Treatment Program
for Bulimia

As we saw in the last chapter, research findings suggest that cognitive–behavioral therapy, including response prevention of vomiting under therapist supervision, is the most effective treatment for bulimia presently available. In this chapter, a 15-session cognitive–behavioral treatment program including response prevention of purging, based on the research findings to date, is presented. The format provided is for individual therapy, although it could easily be adapted to a group format. In the latter case, a group size between 4 and 10 participants is suggested, with two therapists for the larger group. In the later phases of therapy, when in-session response prevention of vomiting is used, the larger group might be split into two smaller groups, each led by one therapist.

Because bulimia is far more common in females than in males, we use the female pronoun throughout when referring to patients. It is also assumed that the assessment procedures described in chapter 2 will have been followed before beginning therapy.

THE TREATMENT PROGRAM

The core procedures used throughout therapy include:

1. Self-monitoring of food intake, binge eating, and vomiting as indicated for each session. Accurate record keeping and careful analysis of these records by the participant and therapist form the basis for therapy.
2. Recording the weekly totals of binge eating and purging on a graph, so that progress in enhancing self-control can be seen by the participant.
3. Disclosure of the eating problem to significant others.

4. The cornerstone of this therapeutic approach is the establishment of a normal eating pattern, including eating three meals each day, with a more normal eating style, healthy food choices, and lessened avoidance of specific foods such as sweets. Recent research shows that even following cognitive–behavioral treatment, considerable restriction of caloric intake still obtains (Kirkley, Agras, & Weiss, 1985). Because this is likely to be associated with relapse, the instigation of normal eating patterns and a less-restricted diet should be attended to throughout therapy.

5. A second major emphasis is the focus on problem solving and the offering of specific behavior-change suggestions to overcome particular problems. Cognitive distortions often impede behavior change, and such distortions should be challenged and more rational alternatives substituted throughout therapy.

6. In later sessions, binge eating and purging behaviors will be focused upon specifically, using an in-session minibinge and between-session practice of response prevention. This procedure allows the therapist to directly confront the participant's faulty beliefs associated with the binge eating and purging patterns. Such beliefs should be explored, clarified, challenged, and reframed with more rational substitutes. The use of other methods to delay vomiting, such as the relaxation response, will also be explored in this condition.

7. In the later phases of therapy there should be an exploration of the antecedents of binge eating and purging, and attention should be paid to increasing assertiveness or other interpersonal problems, if necessary.

8. Finally, relapse prevention procedures should be introduced during the last few sessions.

Session 1

The main aim of the first session is to establish a therapeutic relationship with the patient, and to present and discuss the rationale underlying this approach to treatment. This should begin with the taking of a more detailed history of the participant's condition, demonstrating the expert understanding of the problem by the therapist. If self-monitoring of eating and purging behavior was asked for at the assessment session, this should be examined in detail. This is also an opportunity for the participant to disclose painful and secretive aspects of her behavior to the therapist, beginning a process of desensitization in preparation for self-disclosure to significant others.

Details of past treatment should also be obtained, and any unrealistic expectations of the participant vis-à-vis therapy should be dealt with. Such expectations might include over-optimism, or, given past failures, an undue pessimism. Patients should be reminded that treatment will take place in 15 sessions spread over 17 weeks, and that it will proceed in stages. Their binge/purge pattern will not resolve itself instantly. Given a reasonable degree of behavior change on the part of the participant, the binge/purge behavior should gradually lessen over the 17-week treatment period.

The rationale for treatment should now be outlined along the following lines: standards for physical attractiveness, particularly for women, vary over time. At times a full and rounded figure is desirable, at other times a thin body is the ideal. At present, a very thin body shape is portrayed by advertisers and by the media as most desirable. Because being physically attractive is rewarding, especially for women, some individuals attempt to alter their body shape to a thinner figure. Unfortunately, socially set standards are not always biologically appropriate. Many women naturally have fuller and more rounded figures.

Nonetheless, because of these social pressures for thinness many women begin to diet, often following over-rigorous dietary regimens. Some foods regarded as fattening, such as candies and desserts, are assiduously avoided. Typically, little breakfast or lunch is eaten, as the fear of weight gain, even small gains, increases. This in turn sets up the temptation to binge because of hunger. Sometimes an emotional upset or feelings of depression trigger a binge. Because of the deprivation involved, the binge tends to be on "forbidden and avoided" foods. In turn, this excessive intake of calories tends to lead to weight gain, thus setting up the need to purge. Binge eating simple carbohydrates may lead at first to a feeling of relaxation. But soon the feeling of fullness and fear of weight gain leads to the wish to purge. Purging in turn, combined with a restricted diet, leads inexorably to uncontrollable hunger, thus setting up the next binge. So the binge/purge cycle continues.

Complicating all this is the way in which many bulimics think. Often "all or nothing" thinking leads to trouble. Eating a small amount of "forbidden food" leads to the thought "I've done it now, I might as well go ahead and binge." Accompanying the binge eating and purging cycle is a pervasive feeling of being out of control, which in turn leads to guilt and depression. This feeling of being out of control often extends to other areas of the bulimic's life, leading to demoralization and depression.

Although purging gives individuals the feeling that they have eliminated the calories that they consumed in a binge, this is not so. A considerable number of calories are absorbed before purging occurs. Even laxative use does not eliminate many calories. Typically, when the bulimic gives up purging, only a little weight is gained, and much of the weight gain is not fat, but water, because the bulimic, due to vomiting or laxative use, is always a little dehydrated.

Treatment is aimed at reversing this pathological process. Self-monitoring eating patterns eliminates the avoidance of looking at what is going on. Instead of a hazy notion about the problem, the details are faced more realistically. It also allows us to make specific behavior change recommendations and to monitor the effects of such recommendations. Telling members of one's family about the eating disorder makes the problem more public and may allow family to be more understanding and helpful about the problem. Eating more normally, that is, three meals a day, begins to control excessive hunger and helps to decrease the probability of binge eating and purging. Paradoxically, by eating more during the day, total caloric intake tends to drop as more and more binges are eliminated. Eating small amounts of candies or sweet foods helps overcome "all or nothing" thinking about binge eating, and to restore a feeling of control over eating. Delaying purging after a binge also increases the sense of control, and may help control both binge eating and purging. By not being starved, one feels physically, mentally, and psychologically better. Much of the guilt, anxiety, and depression lessens as binge eating and purging decreases.

For behavior change to occur, it is essential that the participant practice new behaviors, even if such behaviors appear to be risky in the short run. Because this is often difficult, such new behaviors are broken down into small steps. The therapist's role is to bring his or her expertise in behavior change to bear on the problems identified by self-monitoring. The critical importance of accurate adherence to self-monitoring should be stressed, and the participant reminded that the records will provide the data to guide therapy at every session. It is therefore important to fill out the records when the behavior occurs and to remember to bring the records to each treatment session. This in turn should lead to some emphasis on the need to attend each session and to give plenty of notice of possible interruptions such as vacations or business trips or if the appointment should need changing for any reason.

The therapist should then go over the main outlines of the therapy program, that is, this is a 15-session program in which the patient will be expected to be an active participant. Self-monitoring, which will start with monitoring of food intake, binge eating, and vomiting (see Figure 2.2 for an example of a suitable form), will change as the program unfolds to include different aspects of eating behavior and purging. There will be an initial focus on normalizing eating behavior, particularly working toward three meals a day, and eliminating avoidance of particular foods. As the program progresses, we will ask the participant to bring in small quantities of a binge food and to consume enough to generate the urge to vomit. The participant will then be asked to relax, and the course of the anxiety/discomfort followed as it wanes. This procedure will also allow us to focus directly on the faulty perceptions and thoughts associated with the binge eating and purging behaviors. Later we will use self-monitoring to examine some of the triggers to binge eating and vomiting. The participant should be given ample opportunity to ask any questions about the therapy program. This would also be an opportune time to remind the participant that the records she is keeping are for her own benefit.

Dealing with Family Members. The handling of questions from family members should now be dealt with. The participant should be told that family members occasionally become worried about the patient's progress and call the therapist for information. She should be assured that if this occurs, the therapist will inform the family member that nothing can be discussed without the participant's explicit agreement. Even then, only general information concerning the treatment can be given. It has been our experience that for most patients it is better to separate the family from therapy. Should family problems exist, these can be dealt with later by referral for family therapy. In practice we have found that once the bulimic symptoms are overcome such referral is rarely needed.

Homework. "Monitor food intake, including binge eating, together with self-induced vomiting and laxative use patterns for the next week, and bring the records to the next session."

Session 2

The major aims of this session are:

1. To continue to take a history of the disorder, fostering continued self-disclosure of the details of the eating disorder with accompanying desensitization of guilt and anxiety.
2. To examine the self-monitoring records kept by the participant: first, for compliance to the task, and second, to foster the participant's examination of these records, particularly focusing at this stage of therapy on the pattern of meals consumed.
3. To induce the first attempted behavior changes, namely self-disclosure to significant others and beginning to change meal frequency.
4. To restate and further discuss the rationale for the therapy.

Following the greeting of the participant and asking a general question about how the participant is doing, the process of history taking should continue, perhaps taking off naturally from a report of a concrete aspect of the eating problem or an event reported by the participant. Gentle probing for the historical facts and the fine details of the eating disorder should be accomplished during the first part of this session to facilitate self-disclosure. It is important to determine who in the patient's environment is aware of the binge eating and purging pattern and who is not. Should the patient be hiding the behavior from a significant person in her life, the reasons for this should be explored. It will be found that the patient often has distorted ideas about the consequences of self-revelation. These ideas should be elicited and challenged, and the suggestion made that the patient should disclose the nature of her problem to that person. The perfectionism of bulimics often leads to excessive self-criticism regarding the bulimic behavior and leads them to expect such criticism from others.

Resistance to self-disclosure should be carefully worked through. The therapist should take care to not threaten the patient in any way and to allow emotional reactions to dissipate by moving to more neutral topics. Sometimes a role-playing procedure is helpful. The patient might be asked to assume both her own role and that of the person she is describing her problem to. Usually this leads to the realization that the response from the other person will be less negative than the patient initially feared. It has been our experience that it is rare for a family member or close friend to react critically to such revelations. For the most part, self-disclosure mobilizes social support for the participant.

The second half of the session should focus on the patient's self-monitoring of the previous week, and should include the first suggestions for altering the frequency of eating. At some point during this part of the session the therapist should take the opportunity to restate the rationale for this aspect of therapy, namely, that the reestablishment of a normal eating pattern in terms of frequency of eating and what is eaten is the first step in therapy. Interruption of the starvation/deprivation cycle will in turn lead to reduction in the frequency of binge eating with a corresponding decline in the need to purge. Direct attention to the urge to vomit will be dealt with as a second step in therapy, using the technique of a minibinge.

The latter aspect of treatment often causes the client to feel anxious, feelings that should be fully explored by the therapist. Among the concerns raised by patients are feelings of guilt and anxiety (often expressed as a feeling of foolishness) in binge eating in front of the therapist. The therapist might remind the patient that overcoming such feelings is a part of the self-disclosure process. In addition, patients often feel that they will lose control of eating in front of the therapist. It should be pointed out to the patient that only very small amounts of food will be eaten during these sessions, just enough to provoke the urge to vomit.

The therapist and participant should now examine the self-monitoring record for completeness, inquiring whether anything has been inadvertently left out. Problems with completing the self-monitoring record should be carefully examined and a strategy to cope with such problems worked out. The focus of inquiry should then shift to the patterning of meals. As we have seen, the usual bulimic meal pattern is to eat little breakfast or lunch, which in turn leads to excessive hunger by midafternoon that sets up a high probability of binge eating. Although the therapist may feel free to direct the inquiry in the initial sessions, one aim should be to have the participant become an active partner in problem identification and problem solving. Comments by the patient should be appropriately reinforced with attention and praise, and the participant should be prompted into a further analysis of the observed eating patterns, particularly examining missing meals such as breakfast and lunch. Occasions on which these meals are not missed should be commented upon positively, and the reasons for the difference between days on which such a meal has been consumed and days on which there is no such meal should be examined. The patient should again be reminded of the importance of self-monitoring, because it allows the gathering of data, first to delineate the problems, and second to document progress made in changing behaviors.

This examination should lead to the second prescribed behavior-change effort, namely, adding meals early in the day. The participant should be reminded that a general rule for all behavior change is that a slow start will be more successful than attempting major changes and failing. Because bulimics often engage in all-or-nothing thinking, some patients may respond to a directive to add one meal a day by adding all three meals, a step certain to lead to failure. Thus, the first suggestion should be to begin to increase the number of meals consumed, beginning with adding a single meal each day or even every other day that that participant perceives the easiest to add. This is often the breakfast meal. The patient should be explicitly warned against doing more than this. The present content of the meal should be explored using the self-monitoring record, and foods that might be added without causing undue anxiety should be discovered by discussion with the participant. (In selecting foods, the therapist should bear in mind the eventual aim of having the patient eat a heart-healthy diet as described in chapter 4 in the context of the obesity treatment program.) Again, a gradual approach to adding caloric intake to the meal should be taken.

The therapist should then ask the participant to count the number of episodes of self-induced vomiting and laxative use during the week. (If the week is incomplete for any reason, have the patient recall extra episodes in detail and note on the log.) Then the participant should be shown how to plot the data on a graph of purging episodes. Two copies of this graph should be maintained, one for the patient to keep and one for the therapist. The patient should be reminded that she should bring in her copy of the graph each week, along with the new self-monitoring record. If there is time, this task should lead to a discussion of the participant's definition of a binge, of a normal meal, and of dieting. Again, any irrational cognitions should be noted and challenged by the therapist.

Homework. During the next week the participants should concentrate on monitoring meal frequency and the frequency of self-induced vomiting and laxative use, focusing on what was happening when they failed to eat a meal. In addition, they should begin to add to meal content at the frequency and time agreed on.

Sessions 3–5

The major aims of these three sessions are:

1. To check that the participant has complied with any recommendations regarding self-disclosure of the details of the eating disorder to significant others.

2. To examine the self-monitoring record for compliance, and to deal with any resistance to keeping the record.
3. To continue to shape changes in meal frequency.
4. To continue to make changes in the content of meals eaten, moving toward a heart-healthy diet.

Self-Monitoring and Behavior Change. The main focus of each of these sessions should be on an examination of the weekly self-monitoring record with continued suggestions for altering the frequency of eating and the content of the diet. The first task each week should be for the therapist and participant to examine the record for completeness, asking whether anything has been inadvertently left out. As in previous sessions, the aim should be to have the participant take an active role in problem identification and problem-solving activities.

Patients may, at times, resist bringing the self-monitoring forms to the session. Or they may bring them in but not wish the therapist to see them. This usually appears to be related to an unwillingness to fully disclose the nature of their problem because of embarrassment and guilt. This issue should be explored, challenging any distorted cognitions associated with it, such as perfectionistic thoughts. In addition, a shaping approach gradually leading to full disclosure and sharing of the self-monitoring should be adopted.

At this point in treatment it is often useful to outline a more formal problem-solving strategy to the participant. This includes the following steps: (a) identifying the problem in concrete behavioral terms; (b) listing all the possible solutions; (c) ranking the various solutions for practicality; (d) settling on a particular solution and detailing it; and (e) making a written contract to implement the solution. This problem-solving method should be used whenever it seems appropriate, so that the participant gradually comes to use the method on her own. This method will eventually become an important aspect of the maintenance program.

The first emphasis should be on an examination of the patterning of eating, particularly focusing upon breakfast and lunch. Progress in increasing the frequency of the target meal decided upon during the previous week's session should be reinforced by attention and positive comments. It should be remembered that bulimics often minimize their successes and focus on their failures. The therapist must resist getting caught up in this aspect of the patient's cognitive distortion. When the patient begins a recitation of failures, the therapist should deliberately inquire about successes, even small ones. If some of the days on which a meal should have been consumed were missed, then the reasons for this should be examined by contrasting days on which a meal was consumed and days on which it was not. This will usually entail an inquiry into the antecedents and consequences of skipped meals, as well as the decision-making process involved in missing a meal.

Building upon positive gains, the participant should be encouraged to gradually increase the number of meals consumed. The participant should be involved in deciding which meals to add, and upon the content of the meal, as the next step in the process of moving toward eating at least three meals each day so as to interrupt the starvation/binge cycle. Resistance to the notion of increasing meal frequency should be dealt with by examining and challenging the distorted food rules governing this behavior. The bulimic, for example, often feels that eating even a small amount of food increases the risk of a binge or of gaining weight. The rationale that eating more will decrease the likelihood of being very hungry, which is the antecedent event to many binges, should be stressed. By eating three meals a day and not binge eating, the client will be taking in fewer calories than if she starves and binges, because many of the "binge calories" are absorbed before purging is completed.

Meal content focusing both on the restricted caloric intake and the restricted choice of foods that is so typical of this group of participants should be examined in more detail as the frequency of meals increases. The therapist should identify a specific problem area and begin to elaborate a discussion of what could be done about it, for example, adding more food or new food groups to a particular meal. Using a shaping process, the therapist should suggest that the participant identify and add foods that are feared only a little. As these issues are addressed it is likely that some of the participant's distorted cognitions and food rules will become apparent; these perceptions should be firmly and consistently challenged with the aim of substituting more realistic rules.

For example, the bulimic often feels that rigorous dieting is the only way to maintain her weight at a low level. Eating one piece of forbidden food, such as a small slice of cake or a cookie, means that she will gain weight, so she might as well go ahead and binge. Sometimes this idea is elaborated into "I must eat more so that it will be easier for me to induce vomiting and get rid of the forbidden food." The following are corrective statements that might be used in this case: Excessive dieting leads to binge eating, which means taking in a large number of calories that cannot possibly be eliminated. A small piece of cake, the original cause of the problem, will not cause weight gain. Eating it should be an enjoyable experience.

Reductions in vomiting, which should begin during these sessions, should be reinforced and should be tied in with the progress the patient is making in changing her eating patterns and the way she thinks. Should a client report weight gain following a decrease in purging frequency, the therapist could use several responses that may be productive. First, remind the client that a major portion of the weight gain represents an increase in water retention with rehydration. It is not fat. Second, inform the client that clinical experience suggests that few bulimics gain substantial amounts of weight as they progress. Third, emphasize that small weight gains must be viewed in the broader context of improving health and well-being through gradual behavior change. It may be helpful for the bulimic to concentrate less upon weight than upon the way they look to themselves. Bulimics also often focus on atypical negative feedback. If the participant, for instance, reports initial comments from others such as "Looks like you've gained some weight," explore the precise details of the episode. Who actually said what, and how frequently? Ask if, on the other hand, the participant has received any positive feedback recently. Typically, the client will minimize the positive and overemphasize the negative feedback. Help the client to observe this tendency.

During the fifth session the rationale for the introduction of relaxation practice at the next session should be outlined. "Within a couple of sessions we will be introducing the eating of small amounts of binge food during the session. The relaxation exercise will be used to combat the anxiety and discomfort that is induced by this procedure. In addition, relaxation increases the ability to observe feelings and thoughts induced by the experience. The relaxation procedure may also be helpful in delaying binge eating by reducing anxiety." A beginning discussion should be held as to what type of binge food might be brought into Session 7. The basic principle is that only a small amount of food should be brought in, and at first it should not be extremely anxiety-provoking food. Typical foods are a chocolate bar, ice cream, cake, or cookies.

Session 6

The main aims of this session are:

1. To continue to focus on changing meal frequency and content toward a more normal eating style.
2. To introduce and hold a practice relaxation session in preparation for the first response-prevention session to be held next week.
3. To give final instructions regarding response prevention.

The session should begin with a review of adherence to the contract to make changes in the frequency of meals and/or the content of the food consumed (focusing on areas such as broadening food choices, eating a reasonable amount of food for breakfast and lunch, adding small amounts of avoided foods). This should be done by examining the week's self-monitoring. Any attempt to make changes, or any small successes, should be identified by the therapist and reinforced by noting the change and by the judicious use of praise that is clearly contingent upon the successful changes. It should be remembered that bulimics are often self-defeating, relating positive occurrences in a negative manner. Such statements should be reframed to underline the successful element.

This should lead naturally to a discussion of any problems that have been encountered in making the changes, either in meal frequency or in food content. One or two well-specified problem areas should be identified and the participant should be encouraged to develop a concrete plan to solve the problems. Such plans will probably make use of the principle of gradual change, adding, for example, a small amount of a new food group or a slightly greater number of calories to a particular meal, especially breakfast or lunch.

The new material for this week should then be introduced. This should consist of a rationale for the use of the relaxation exercise as a stress-management procedure to overcome anxiety that might provoke binge eating, as a technique that will be used to overcome the anxiety provoked by response prevention of vomiting, and as a useful technique to use to delay vomiting once binge eating has occurred. Then, the relaxation procedure should be briefly described, that is, learning to relax tense muscles and to attain mental calm. The evidence that relaxation leads to lowered physiologic arousal (for example, in blood pressure, heart rate, tense muscles as in a tension headache, and all aspects of anxiety) should be briefly stated. The tension–relaxation exercises for specific muscle groups should then be briefly demonstrated following the instructions on the patient handout (see Appendix C).

A relaxation practice should then be held using the tape that will be given to the patient to practice with.* During this part of the session the therapist should observe the patient and correct any faulty tension–relaxation exercises, breathing, posture, etc. However, the main emphasis should be upon attaining a reasonable state of comfort and relaxation. Following completion of the relaxation exercises, the therapist should ask about any positive changes noted while relaxing. Participants often will remark that they have never felt so relaxed or that a specific tension symptom has been relieved. Such changes should be commented upon in a positive way, adding to the expectancy that continued practice of the exercises will make it even easier to attain a state of calm and to overcome anxiety. If little tension relief was experienced, the therapist should emphasize that practice of the exercise will lead to increased ability to cope with tension. The therapist should also inquire into any problems that the patient may be experiencing while attempting to relax, such as intrusive thoughts. He or she should give the patient specific instructions as to how to cope with such problems: for example, simply letting the thought go by without elaborating on it or using a simple counting mantra to help refocus on the relaxation procedure.

The rationale for response prevention should now be reiterated, namely, that the only way to overcome the purging behavior is to face the irrational fear of gaining weight by eating feared foods without purging. Doing this while noting the absence of deleterious consequences will allow the anxiety to dissipate. Note that the participant should bring a small amount of binge food to the next session, but that only enough will be eaten to provoke a small amount of anxiety.

Of course, it is possible that the participant will have ceased purging by this point in therapy and may wonder why response prevention should be engaged in. It is important to note that it is the anxiety associated with the consumption of binge foods that response prevention is aimed at. It is very unlikely that such anxiety has dissipated by this point in therapy. In any event, this is an empirical

---

*See Ferguson, Marquis, & Taylor, 1977, for an example of a script for relaxation practice.

question that can be solved by having the participant consume increasing amounts of binge food over the next few sessions.

Wilson (1985) has suggested that a videotape of a person describing their success with in-session binge eating and response prevention should be shown to the bulimic at this point. This procedure makes good sense, because such previews based on vicarious learning have been shown to be useful in other problem areas, particularly with phobias of various kinds.

Session 7

This session should begin with the minibinge to allow time for the anxiety provoked by binge eating to dissipate before the end of the session. Following the instructions from last week's session, the patient should have brought a small quantity of the least disturbing binge food with her to the session. Participants will occasionally "forget" to bring the food, or be "unable" to obtain it. In this case, the anxiety surrounding the minibinge should be explored and distorted cognitions challenged. In some cases, having to eat binge food in front of someone is the disturbing aspect, often accompanied by massive guilt. In other cases, the anxiety may be that the participant will lose control of eating in the session, binge eating to the point of needing to purge at once. More rational alternatives should be put to the patient in each case.

The rationale given during the last session regarding the purpose of a minibinge should be reiterated, namely, that binge eating is partly maintained by purging and that if control over purging is gained, binge eating will not be as likely to occur. The therapy sessions are designed to allow patients to get in touch with the distorted thoughts and feelings provoked by eating feared foods. This will allow them to better tolerate such anxiety without resorting to vomiting and to think more rationally about the consumption of feared foods.

The purpose of this part of the session is to replicate, in a tolerable way, the discomfort consequent upon consuming binge food. Such discomfort will be experienced in different ways by different individuals, including feelings of bloating, shame or guilt, anxiety, or the urge to vomit. The aim of this first session is to create only a small amount of discomfort, and then to tolerate that discomfort without vomiting either during or after the session. The expectation should be given that the discomfort will slowly disappear, and with it the need to induce purging. The relaxation exercises that were practiced during the week will be used to help diminish the discomfort due to eating feared foods.

The therapist should take this opportunity to examine the self-monitoring records of relaxation practice, including the reductions in tension following the exercise. Positive changes should be commented upon, and their usefulness in reducing the discomfort associated with consuming binge food pointed out. The overall response to relaxation training seems to be positive in this group of patients. Some use the procedure for stress reduction, finding it helpful in handling the antecedent events to binge eating in a better way. Others use relaxation to delay binge eating and/or self-induced vomiting. A few patients find the procedure uncomfortable and do not follow through on practice. For these patients, simply sitting in a chair, with or without closing their eyes, will suffice for the conduct of the minibinge.

The method used to indicate amount of discomfort and the urge to vomit should then be discussed with the patient, and she should be asked to report her present level of discomfort from 0 to 10, with 0 being perfectly comfortable and 10 being intolerable discomfort. The patient should then be encouraged to eat a portion of binge food, but in this first session only to the point of inducing mild discomfort. The all-or-nothing tendency of bulimics to overdo things should be guarded against by limiting the patient to a small amount of food for this first session so that the patient's responses can be directly observed by the therapist. Sometimes participants will apparently be comfortable eating a large amount of food, after which anxiety suddenly builds to intolerable levels. This situation should be avoided by setting limits on the amount of food consumed in the first session or two and then gradually increasing the amount and type of food consumed. Following the eating of some binge food, the patient should be asked to report her level of discomfort and urge to vomit. A relaxation session should then be started.

During the relaxation session the degree of discomfort and urge to vomit should be checked every few minutes. Decreases in discomfort should be verbally reinforced, and a discussion of the patient's ability to delay vomiting initiated. Thoughts and feelings about the binge and about not vomiting should be elicited, faulty cognitions should be challenged, and more rational substitutes offered by the therapist.

Among these cognitions may be the following:

1. Guilt or shame at having eaten "so much food." (The participant should be reminded that the actual amount of food eaten was in fact small and contained few calories.)
2. Distorted physical sensations of bloating and swelling of stomach, thighs, and hips after eating only a small amount of food. (It is impossible for such changes to occur. This is an example of catastrophic thinking and of distortion of the normal feeling of fullness and comfort after eating.)
3. The absolute need to vomit to relieve such feelings, even though only a small amount of food has been consumed. Usually this is accompanied by a fear of weight gain. (It is not possible for weight to be gained from eating a small amount of food.)
4. Having broken a "food rule," they *must* vomit (all-or-nothing thinking).

When the discomfort and urge to vomit has dissipated enough to allow more discussion, the therapist should review the self-monitoring records from the previous week. The first aim should be to monitor adherence to the contract to make changes in the frequency and content of food consumed (focusing on areas such as increasing the frequency of meals to at least three per day, broadening food choices, and adding avoided foods). Any attempt to make changes or any small successes should be identified by the therapist and reinforced by noting the change, and by the judicious use of praise. Problems encountered in making the changes, either in meal frequency or in food content, should be discussed and new goals for change made.

Homework for the Next Week. This includes the following:

1. Continue to practice with the relaxation tape 5 to 7 times each week.
2. Use the relaxation procedure to delay purging (even minimally) on more than one occasion during the next week and keep track of discomfort levels during this exercise, using the forms provided.
3. Continue to work on increasing meal regularity and changing meal content in a positive way during the next week.
4. Self-monitor binge eating and purging frequencies.
5. Remind the participant to bring more binge food with her to the next session.

Sessions 8–12

The main aim of these sessions is to continue the in-session minibinge with prevention of vomiting, to begin response-prevention practice in the home, to introduce relevant changes in eating style, to examine the antecedent social contributors to binge eating, and to follow up on meal frequency and meal content changes.

The first task of each session should be to hold the in-session minibinge. As the discomfort concerning the eating of binge foods without purging dissipates with successive sessions, the participant should be encouraged to bring in more difficult food items to consume, and then increasing quantities of the more difficult items. The session should be conducted as previously described, continuing to challenge unrealistic thoughts and feelings uncovered during the minibinge.

As the patient becomes more comfortable with the in-session minibinge, the therapist should discuss with her the possibility of setting up home practice of response prevention. Such practice might be set up with the help of a relative or friend, or alternatively, the patient might practice on her own. Exactly the same food should be used in the home practice as was used in the therapist's office. At first only one such session should be held each week, but as time goes on the frequency can be increased. In addition, the patient should increasingly use alternative and incompatible activities to delay and eliminate purging occurring after binge eating. Such activities include use of the relaxation tape, going for a walk, or talking to a friend on the telephone.

This is also an appropriate time to begin to make changes in the binge eating behavior itself. Usually, binge food is rapidly eaten, often directly from cartons, and often under particular circumstances such as watching television, standing in the kitchen, or sitting in an automobile. Rarely is binge food consumed as part of a regularly scheduled meal, or under the circumstances in which meals are usually eaten, such as sitting at a table with a place setting. Following a careful analysis of the circumstances surrounding binge eating, the patient should be encouraged to make the following alterations: eating binge food at a table with a place setting, and sitting down; eating the binge food from a plate and with utensils; eating slowly, counting each bite of food; changing the room or other circumstances in which a binge usually takes place.

Suggestions for such changes may meet with considerable resistance from the patient. Changes, therefore, should be made gradually, and the patient should be encouraged to take the risks associated with making such changes. Quite dramatic shifts in binge eating are often noted after altering the circumstances in which it occurs. For example, one patient who binge ate in front of the television found that when she turned the set off, she became aware of the street noises and of people on the street outside her apartment. This awareness decreased her sense of loneliness that had accompanied binge eating and decreased her urge.

In some patients, self-induced vomiting can be approached in a similar way. The induction of vomiting is often carried out in a set manner. For example, the wash basin tap might be run to cover up the noise of vomiting, the patient may drape a towel around her to avoid messing her clothing, and she may clean up in a particular way after vomiting. Following a detailed analysis of the circumstances surrounding vomiting, the patient should be encouraged to drop out elements of the ritual. Again, this should be done slowly and with much reinforcement for success.

The social antecedents of binge eating should also be examined more thoroughly during these sessions. For some patients, almost every affect and situation can be associated with binge eating, and there is little specific to work on. For others, binge eating occurs in quite specific circumstances. For example, binge eating followed by self-induced vomiting occurred for one of our patients only when she was angry at her husband. Moreover, the situation from which the anger stemmed, being put down in some way by her husband, was consistent from time to time. In this case, therapy was directed toward increasing this patient's assertiveness and communication skills, so that she felt put down less often in the interchanges between her husband and herself.

Finally, it has proven helpful for some patients, who have successfully reduced binge eating and vomiting but have not eliminated these behaviors, to begin to contract to reduce the number each week, finally setting a quit date. This is similar to the way in which many cigarette-cessation programs are conducted. Again, the patient has to be encouraged to take the risk of stopping vomiting, to prove to herself that nothing deleterious, such as putting on large amounts of weight, is going to happen to her.

Sessions 13–15

The main aims of these sessions are:

1. To continue the in-session minibinges as appropriate to the individual case, together with practice at home and attention to decreasing steps in the vomiting ritual.
2. To identify and work on residual problem areas.
3. To address the issue of relapse and relapse prevention.

It is suggested that the remaining sessions should be held 2 weeks apart, allowing for a more gradual attenuation of the therapeutic relationship, and for the patient to become more independent of the therapist and to assume greater responsibility for problem identification and for behavior change. After completing the in-session minibinge (if it should prove necessary at this stage of therapy), the therapist should conduct an overall review of progress in therapy, aimed at identifying the most important remaining problems and working out plans to deal with them. The various areas of behavior change should be outlined and progress in each of them reviewed. These include self-disclosure, regularity of meals, content of food eaten—moving toward a heart-healthy diet and overcoming restricted dietary content—introducing "forbidden" foods, changing eating style both in normal eating and in binges, response-prevention generalization training, delay of vomiting, and coping with precipitating stressors.

A list of residual problems should be developed and the participant encouraged to rank them in order of personal importance. One or two of these problems should be chosen to be worked upon during the remaining weeks of therapy. A careful behavior analysis of each of the problems should be performed, focusing both upon the difficulties encountered in changing the behaviors in question and on the building up of new or alternative behaviors. Self-monitoring should therefore concentrate on the behaviors chosen for change.

In subsequent sessions, the therapist should review the participant's progress in reducing the residual problem behavior. Success should be praised and residual problems should be carefully analyzed. The therapist should encourage the participant to develop a plan for the next several weeks to help overcome the particular residual problem. In this exercise, it is useful to remind the patient of the formal problem-solving strategy that should be used: (a) identify the problem in concrete terms; (b) use self-monitoring to identify the frequency of the problem; (c) list all potential coping strategies; (d) choose a coping strategy and institute it; (e) use self-monitoring to record changes in the problem behavior; and (f) if the problem behavior is not diminishing after 1 week, start back at (d). Should the problem(s) have been overcome between sessions, a new problem or problems should be chosen from the list of residual problems.

Again, the participant should be urged to develop a plan to deal with the problem.

Finally, the participant should be reminded that she will need to begin to think about what to do in the case of relapse during the next several months. Some form of lapse should be expected, and it is very important to pick up the early signs of such relapse. The rationale for relapse prevention includes the notion that there are two aims of this phase of treatment: to prevent the occurrence of an initial lapse into binge eating and self-induced vomiting; and should that occur, to prevent the lapse from extending into a full-scale and continuing relapse. One goal is to enhance the patient's expectation concerning her capacity to deal with high-risk situations by pointing out that the longer that abstinence continues, the greater is the demonstrated capacity to cope with increasingly high-risk situations. Thus the sense of personal control deepens as time goes by without a relapse.

The probable early signs of relapse should be discussed with the participant, as should the coping techniques to be used. One way to do this is to use the technique of visualization of high-risk situations that might provoke a relapse as described in the protocol for the treatment of obesity (see chapter 4). As noted previously, the antecedent events to binge eating and purging are very often mood states; thus, it is important to have the patient monitor such states at some point during treatment. Strategies that have worked during treatment to extend control over high-risk situations should be reviewed with the patient, and the patient should be encouraged to make up a list of such strategies. The list should be further reviewed and the techniques critiqued for their applicability at this stage of treatment, ending up with a list ordered in terms of usefulness. Items on the list might include behaviors incompatible with binge eating and vomiting, such as going out for a walk, telephoning a friend, going out with a friend, and so on.

Should relapse occur, self-monitoring should be reinstated, paying particular attention to basic behaviors such as meal frequency, meal content, and eating style. Problems should be identified as previously discussed, and the patient's ability to successfully identify and cope with such problems, using the problem-solving technique, should be pointed out.

Various forms of follow-up are possible once the initial series of sessions has been completed. These include scheduled telephone calls at increasing intervals and short follow-up visits. At these times, the patient's success should be reinforced and help with any residual problems offered, by aiding the patient in problem identification and problem solving. A recently completed follow-up study suggests that the highest risk time for relapse is in the 6 months following completion of therapy. After that time, eating behavior appeared to become stable (Luka, Agras, & Schneider, 1986).

OTHER AVAILABLE BULIMIA
TREATMENT PROGRAMS

Treating Bulimia: A Psychoeducational Approach.
Lillie Weiss, Melanie Katzman, Sharlene Wolchik.

This 109-page guidebook outlines a seven-session group-treatment program for bulimia. The program is derived from the basic literature on bulimia. A report of a controlled comparison with no treatment recently appeared (Wolchick, Weiss, & Katzman, 1986). As discussed in the previous chapter, this treatment package seems less powerful than cognitive–behavioral treatment. Nonetheless, this is an interesting book, going into detail regarding affective and cognitive components of bulimia, cultural expectations, and body-image problems. This book can be ordered through Pergamon Press.

Chapter 7
The Treatment of Anorexia Nervosa

As is the case for obesity and bulimia, the two treatment approaches to anorexia nervosa for which the best research basis exists are behavioral and pharmacologic, although the place of the latter in treatment is not entirely clear. Moreover, most treatment programs contain procedures that have not been tested in controlled clinical trials. Most therapists agree that there are two stages to the treatment of the anorexic patient: first, restoration of body weight to as near normal as possible, usually accomplished in a specialized inpatient setting; and second, longer-term therapy directed toward preventing relapse.

Unfortunately, the relative rarity of anorexia nervosa has retarded the development of a scientifically based approach to treatment, because between-group outcome studies with sufficient statistical power are extraordinarily difficult to carry out (Agras & Kraemer, 1983). Thus, although there have been studies of the treatment of anorexia nervosa, all have been short term and directed toward the restoration of normal weight. Longer-term treatment is based entirely upon clinical experience. Few well-documented treatment approaches to this phase of therapy exist. Nonetheless, using analagous approaches to the treatment of bulimia, a cognitive–behavioral approach to the treatment of anorexia nervosa has been described in some detail (Garner, Garfinkel, & Bemis, 1982).

BEHAVIORAL APPROACHES

The major behavioral approach to the treatment of anorexia nervosa uses reinforcement theory in an inpatient setting to motivate patients to gain weight. This method was first described in 1965 (Bachrach, Erwin, & Mohr, 1965). These workers treated a severely emaciated 37-year-old woman who weighed 21.4 kg on admission to hospital, a drop of some 32.2 kg from her normal adult weight. Social reinforcement that included attention, conversation, and praise was made contingent upon eating. To enhance the effects of reinforcement, the patient was placed in a hospital room devoid of amenities such as television, books, or frequent visits from the nursing and medical staff and visitors. Reinforcer deprivation of this sort has been shown to enhance the effects of contingent reinforcement on performance.

The first procedure used consisted of the therapist sitting with the patient at every meal and conversing with her only when she ate. Conversation and praise were used to shape an approximately normal eating rate. Other reinforcers, such as going for walks or visits from relatives, were also made contingent upon satisfactory eating behavior. The patient gained some 7 kg with this regimen and then her weight leveled off. At this point, the therapists suspected that she was vomiting her food after eating. Reinforcement then was made contingent upon weight gain, rather than upon eating behavior. This is evidently a superior contingency because it insures both a reasonable caloric intake and the reduction of self-induced vomiting. Unfortunately, the effect of this change in contingencies was not clear because the patient was discharged too soon after it was introduced to evaluate its effectiveness.

Subsequent case reports appeared to confirm the finding that reinforcement contingencies applied to weight gain were successful in helping anorexic patients to gain weight. For the most part, privileges of various kinds have been made contingent upon small increments of weight gain over the previous highest weight. Some interesting variations have, however, been reported. In one study, the well-known reinforcing properties of physical exercise for the anorexic patient were used to advantage (Blinder, Freeman, & Stunkard, 1970). These investigators made access to physical activity contingent upon weight gain, reporting marked success in three patients. In yet another variation on this theme, the activity of another anorexic patient was restricted by using chlorpromazine in sedative doses. Increments of drug dose were removed, dependent upon weight gain, thus allowing increases in activity levels contingent upon weight increase.

Despite these initial successes in uncontrolled case studies, the first experimental analysis of the use of positive reinforcement in anorexia nervosa revealed some rather puzzling results (Agras, Barlow, Chapin, Abel, & Leitenberg, 1974). In this experiment, an anorexic patient was served 6,000 calories per day, divided into three meals and an evening snack. Meals lasted for 30 minutes and were eaten alone, being served and removed without comment regarding the amount eaten by the nursing staff. Three experimental phases were held: a baseline condition, a reinforcement phase, and a return to baseline. During the baseline condition, in order to have the patient attend to the process of recovery and to feel motivated, she was asked to record the number of mouthfuls of food that she ate at each meal and to plot these data on a graph kept in plain sight on the wall of her room.

Reinforcement consisted of praise and social attention for eating more, as measured by mouthfuls and by caloric intake, the latter being provided to the patient each day, and for weight gain. In addition, pleasurable activities such as time outside her room and walks with a nurse were made contingent upon small increments of weight gain. The introduction of reinforcement led to rapid increases in caloric intake and a corresponding increase in weight. Reinforcement was then removed in a return to the baseline conditions. Remarkably, caloric intake remained stable and weight gain continued despite the absence of reinforcement. Two replications of this experiment with different patients revealed similar results. These findings suggested that although contingent reinforcement was responsible for the beginning weight gain, another variable was responsible for continued weight gains.

On inquiry, each of these patients claimed that once they realized that they could gain weight, they continued to eat in order to be able to leave hospital, an environment that they had come to dislike because of the various restrictions on their behavior. This, of course, is an example of negative reinforcement, in which an individual behaves in a particular way in order to remove an aversive event or situation from their personal environment. To nullify the effect of negative reinforcement in subsequent experiments, and to examine the effect of positive reinforcement uncomplicated by negative reinforcement, a contract was negotiated with the participant and her parents, such that the participant would remain in hospital for 12 weeks for the purposes of research, whether or not she gained weight during that time. In this way the effect of negative reinforcement was removed, because it was not possible for the patient to leave the hospital by gaining weight.

The effects of this new contingency were quite clear. In contrast with the previous experiments, when positive reinforcement for weight gain was removed the patient's caloric intake and weight dropped. By removing the obscuring effect of negative reinforcement, the effect of removing positive reinforcement was clarified. We therefore can conclude that both positive and negative reinforcement lead to weight gain in the anorexic patient.

Another observation during these experiments led to the delineation of two further therapeutic factors. During the baseline condition of the previous experiments, patients tended to increase their caloric intake and weight, yet positive reinforcement had not yet begun. During this phase the patient was served large meals in order to be able to measure caloric intake accurately, and was given feedback as to her weight each day, the number of mouthfuls that she ate at each meal, and her daily caloric intake. Either of these two factors, the large meals or feedback, or both, might have had therapeutic effects.

To investigate the effect of informational feedback, a potentially powerful procedure in behavior change, a new baseline condition devoid of both feedback and reinforcement was instituted. Caloric intake under this condition seemed to be stable. When positive reinforcement was begun in the next phase, without the addition of feedback, no effect was observed on caloric intake or weight. When feedback was added in the next phase, the patient began to eat more and to gain weight. Removal of feedback led to weight loss. Thus, neither feedback (as shown in the baseline phases of previous experiments) nor reinforcement by themselves lead to major weight gain. It is the combination of reinforcement and feedback that has the best therapeutic effects.

Finally, the effect of serving large meals was investigated. It was found that the intake of anorexic patients was always lowered by some 500 calories per day when smaller meals were served, even though the anorexic never ate all the food served to her at any one meal (Agras et al., 1974; Elkin, Hersen, Eisler, & Williams, 1973). These four procedures, positive and negative reinforcement, informational feedback, and the serving of large meals, form the basis of a therapeutic approach to the in-hospital treatment of anorexia nervosa that will be described in detail later in this chapter.

Only one large-scale clinical trial of the effects of behavior therapy as compared to mileu therapy has been reported (Eckert, Goldberg, Casper, & Halmi, 1979). This study involved 81 anorexic young women who participated in this experiment for 35 days. Only the initial effects of the different treatments were investigated in this study. Forty patients were allocated at random to behavior therapy and 41 to milieu therapy. The weight gains at 35 days were not significantly different between these two groups. It did appear, however, that patients who had received no previous outpatient therapy responded better to behavior therapy than those who had been previously treated. This finding suggests that behavior therapy might be particularly applicable to the less complicated case of anorexia nervosa.

PHARMACOLOGIC APPROACHES

Research on the use of pharmacologic agents to treat patients with anorexia nervosa also suffers from the relative rarity of the condition, leading again to the use of small sample sizes and, for the most part, to uncertain findings. Two classes of drugs have received the most attention to date, antidepressants, such as amitriptyline hydrochloride, a tricyclic antidepressant; and appetite stimulants such as cyproheptadine hydrochloride. The use of antidepressant medication stems from the observation that most anorexic patients appear to be depressed, thus, treatment of this depression may be accompanied by the increase in appetite and weight gain that is seen in the depressed patient when treated with such agents. It is also possible, however, that such depression is secondary to the metabolic disturbances induced by weight loss and that depressive symptoms will improve as weight is gained.

In one controlled trial, 16 anorexic patients were randomly allocated to receive either the antidepressant agent clomipramine or a placebo (Lacey & Crisp, 1980). The difference in weight gain between these two groups was not statistically significant; indeed, there was a trend for the placebo group to gain weight more quickly than the drug group. On the other hand, appetite and caloric intake were both greater in the group receiving active medication. The reason for the slower weight gain in the clomipramine group may have been increased activity. Lithium carbonate, which has also been shown to have anti-depressant properties, particularly in manic–depressive psychosis, has also been used to treat anorexia nervosa (Gross et al., 1981). In this study, 16 anorexics were allocated at random to receive either lithium carbonate or a pla-cebo, with both groups participating in a behavior therapy program. Lithium levels between 0.9 and 1.4 mgm per liter were attained during the 4-week trial. The group receiving lithium gained significantly more weight than that receiv-ing placebo. However, baseline caloric intake was significantly higher for those who afterwards received lithium (2,345 calories) than for those who received the placebo (1,569 calories). The difference is particularly problematic because of the small sample size and short duration of treatment used, for it may well have accounted for the apparently greater effectiveness of lithium. Both of these studies underscore another difficulty in designing clinical outcome studies in anorexia nervosa. In both studies, pharmacological therapy was added to ongo-ing therapeutic programs that have been shown to lead to weight gain. To dem-onstrate an effect of a pharmacologic agent over and above the effects of another active treatment requires an even larger sample size than that needed to com-pare a drug with a placebo. Thus, it is quite possible that the effects of drugs are underestimated in such studies.

The most impressive pharmacological study, comparing the effects of ami-triptyline hydrochloride and cyproheptadine in the treatment of anorexia ner-vosa, was recently published (Halmi, Eckert, LaDu, & Cohen, 1986). Seventy-two anorexic patients were randomly allocated in a double blind study to one of three conditions: amitriptyline, cyproheptadine, or a placebo. The maximal daily dose for amitriptyline was 160 mg, and for cyproheptadine, 32 mg. Patients were maintained on the highest dose of medication that they were able to tolerate. Patients were regarded as treatment failures if they had not gained 2 kg after 6 weeks of treatment. This study was carried out at three coop-erating centers. One of the problems of multicenter studies was immediately apparent, namely, that there was a significant between-center difference in the outcome of treatment, presumably due to differences in the ward mileu.

The major finding from this study stemmed from the comparison between bulimic and nonbulimic anorexics. Cyproheptadine was significantly superior to the placebo in terms of time taken to reach goal weight for the nonbulimic anorexic patient, but seemed to retard recovery in the bulimic anorexic. Ami-triptyline appeared to have borderline effects in the anorexic patient, and the investigators note the difficulty that patients have in tolerating the side effects of this medication.

This is a particularly interesting study because it supports the differentiation between the restricting anorexic and the bulimic anorexic that was discussed in chapter 2. Moreover, the trends in improvement for amitriptyline are also in line with this distinction, with the bulimic anorexic tending to respond better than the nonbulimic to this medication, as we might expect from the pharmacologic studies of less severe bulimics discussed in chapter 5. Because baseline weight was shown in one study to predict outcome in the bulimic treated with imipramine (that is, the lower the weight the poorer the outcome), we might expect the results of antidepressant treatment to be less impressive in the lower weight, more severe (anorexic) bulimic patient. Such a differential effect of medication further compounds the sample size problems in outcome studies of anorexia nervosa.

We can conclude from these studies that only cyproheptadine has been shown to be useful in the treatment of anorexia nervosa, and only for the nonbulimic case. The drug should not be prescribed for the bulimic anorexic because it appears to retard recovery. Other medication should only be used for a specific indication in the treatment of anorexia nervosa, including those cases in which the degree of depression appears to be affecting the rate of recovery. For such cases the use of an antidepressant agent should be considered. It should, however, be remembered that improvement in depression seems to parallel improvement in weight status. For the patient who is able to cooperate with the program and gain weight, the use of an antidepressant agent is not indicated. Because of the side effects experienced by many patients, such an agent may be detrimental to recovery.

CONTROLLED STUDIES OF THE TREATMENT OF OTHER ASPECTS OF ANOREXIA NERVOSA

Given the difficulties in conducting large-scale studies with anorexia nervosa, and the prime importance of ensuring weight gain, it is not surprising that very few studies have been directed toward other aspects of psychopathology such as the behavioral deficits manifested by the anorexic patient. The onset of anorexia nervosa in adolescence, with its accompanying weight loss, leads to a withdrawal from the normal social interactions that occur in this very important period of development. In consequence, much of the social learning that normally takes place in adolescence is not experienced by the anorexic, with subsequent defects in interpersonal behaviors, particularly, perhaps, in a heterosocial context.

This line of reasoning led Pillay and Crisp (1981) to examine the effect of social-skills training in the overall treatment of anorexia nervosa. They randomly allocated 24 patients being treated on an inpatient unit to receive either 12 sessions of social-skills training or none. Four weeks after restoration of normal body weight, no significant change in social skills was found for either group. At 1-year follow-up, the fear of negative evaluation was significantly lower for those receiving social-skills training, but no other differences between the groups were found. These findings suggest that social-skills training had a relatively weak effect upon the generation and acquisitions of social skills in this group of anorexic patients. This type of study points to an important direction for future research, for much of the treatment package used to treat anorexics is based upon clinical experience rather than upon controlled studies. Should well-done studies demonstrate that some or all of these components of therapy were not useful, important savings in the cost of treatment of anorexia nervosa might be made.

INPATIENT TREATMENT: AN OVERVIEW

The ability to take a longer view of the results of treatment is always interesting. To this end, one study pooled from the literature cases of anorexia nervosa that had been presented in sufficient detail to facilitate a numerical approach to the data (Agras & Kraemer, 1983). The first finding was interesting, namely that the admission BMI for anorexic patients has been steadily declining since 1930. Because admission weight is a prognostic indicator for the treatment of anorexia nervosa (the lower the weight, the poorer the outcome), this finding suggests that over time more severe anorexia nervosa cases are being admitted to hospital. This makes comparisons of outcomes over time difficult. Nonetheless, there is no evidence that more modern treatments have increased the weight gain of anorexic patients admitted to hospital.

The authors also compared the efficacy of different kinds of treatment, dividing them into medically oriented therapy (including psychotherapy), behavior therapy, and drug therapy. Patients treated solely with medication appeared to do less well than those in the other two groups in terms of weight gain during hospitalization. This is not entirely surprising because this comparison included many medications that have not been shown to be effective in controlled trials. No difference was found in terms of weight gain between medical therapy and behavior therapy. Behavior therapy, however, was more efficient than medical therapy, in that the length of stay in hospital was significantly shorter than for medical therapy. The rate of weight gain with behavior therapy was significantly superior to that of the other two therapies. This would suggest that behavior therapy should be the preferred approach to the in-hospital care of the anorexic patient, supplemented by the use of cyproheptadine in the restricting anorexic.

Long Term Results of Therapy

Follow-up studies suggest that some two-thirds of previously hospitalized anorexic patients will be at normal or near normal weight, and that the majority of this group of individuals will have resumed regular menstruation. About half the population, however, will continue to have eating difficulties and will show social and psychiatric impairment. Between 2 and 6% of patients will have died from complications of the anorexia, or from suicide (Hsu, 1980). Moreover, the death rate steadily increases as the length of follow-up increases. Follow-ups between 10 and 15 years suggest that the death rate from complications of anorexia nervosa is between 10 and 15%. These results suggest that we have much to learn regarding the long-term treatment of anorexia nervosa.

AN INPATIENT
TREATMENT PROGRAM

Before considering the inpatient approach to the treatment of anorexia nervosa in more detail, it is important to remember that the assessment phase is an important aspect of the treatment of this disorder. The way in which assessment is conducted, and the implicit and explicit agreements made, will affect the course of treatment. The essential contract to be negotiated before entering hospital is that the patient is willing to be hospitalized and that the patient and parents agree that the anorexic will remain in hospital until the patient, both parents, and the treatment team all agree that further hospitalization is not necessary. Coercing the patient to enter the hospital is unwise because the degree of resistance to the treatment program may be inordinate, making it impossible for treatment to proceed. Moreover, the nature of the treatment program and the expectations that the staff will have for the patient and for family members must be clearly explained to both the patient and the family in this phase of treatment.

Time must be taken in the assessment phase to deal with family problems and to negotiate this basic contract. This can be an extremely painful time for the patient, the family, and the therapist. The latter must resist the wish to prematurely force closure on this process. Only a medical emergency should lead to immediate hospitalization, and such an admission should be to a medical unit. It may take many weeks for some patients and their families to agree to the need for hospital care and to the basic treatment contract. Because it is not uncommon for the parents of an anorexic to remove the patient from treatment in spite of the patient having made good progress, it is necessary to involve parents in the formulation of the treatment contract.

The treatment of anorexia nervosa is interdisciplinary in nature, involving psychiatry, psychology, internal medicine, nursing, dietetics, and physical therapy. Such treatment should only take place within a unit that specializes in the care of such patients. However, because of the relative rarity of the disorder, few units devoted solely to the treatment of anorexia nervosa exist. One treatment model is a *behavioral medicine unit* on which psychiatry and medicine share the medical responsibility, while other team members share in the treatment. The mix of patients, who vary in age and sex and have a variety of medical and behavior problems, makes a suitable mileu for the anorexic patient.

The organization of communication between different members of the treatment team is crucial to the success of treatment. Frequent meetings involving the whole team are needed so that each step in therapy can be carefully planned and integrated across the various disciplines involved. Without such meetings, the different disciplines involved in the treatment of the anorexic can work at cross purposes. I have seen a patient being reinforced for weight gain while being served just 1,500 calories each day, not nearly enough food to lead to an increase in weight. Naturally, the patient did not complain about the situation, although the staff were puzzled as to why the patient was showing no response to the contingencies. Such meetings are also needed to stop patients from playing off one staff member against another and to integrate the input from many sources about a particular incident that might have occurred during treatment. Naturally, a team in which the members are in conflict or in competition with one another will not be able to provide adequate care for such the anorexic patient. The role of unit director, someone not directly involved in the day-to-day care of patients, is often crucial in helping to resolve staff conflicts and in maintaining a high morale.

Phases of Therapy

Therapy is organized into four main phases: a baseline adjustment period, the period of weight gain, a maintenance phase, and a posthospital treatment phase. The first phase is usually between 5 and 7 days in length. The longest in-hospital phase is the period of weight gain, aiming at a rate of about 0.2 kg gain per day. For a weight gain of 10 kg, this would require some 50 days in this phase of treatment. The maintenance phase is usually short, perhaps 10 days in length, and is aimed at adjusting eating patterns to a more normal caloric intake and at making the final arrangements for discharge. Outpatient follow-up care, although the least-studied aspect of the treatment of anorexia nervosa, may be the most crucial aspect of treatment, aimed as it is at preventing relapse. Each of these phases will be described in some detail.

The Baseline Phase. This period of time, usually about 5 days in length, is aimed at a thorough assessment of the patient's medical, nutritional, and psychological status. It also allows the patient time to adjust to the unit. It is hoped that the patient will have visited the unit before admission and will have had the program explained in some detail. During this time, patients should attend all the various required ward activities to allow them to feel at ease with the staff and other patients and to accustom them to the various treatment modalities.

One of the main goals of this phase is to work out a treatment contract in some detail. Although the principle is to reinforce small increments of weight gain each day, various methods of achieving this end are possible. In almost all programs there is a "bare bones" contract stipulating access to programmatic activities and to the social amenities offered on the unit contingent on gaining an increment of weight each day above the previous day's high weight. Failure to gain this amount of weight results in restriction to the patient's room. The increment of weight gain is usually set at 0.2 kg/day above the previous high weight. A smaller weight gain, for example 0.1 kg/day, might result in room restriction for half a day. It is, of course, necessary that the patient's room not contain many reinforcing activities. In some units, television and reading material are not allowed in the patients' rooms. In other centers, the entire first phase of weight gain is spent at bed rest, with the rationale that less energy is expended, thus making it easier to gain weight. It should be noted that this use of bed rest is an example of negative reinforcement.

An alternative to the above reinforcement scheme is known as the "line method," in which a line from the patient's baseline weight is drawn on a graph at an increase of 0.2 kg/day. The patient gains access to the privileges associated with the bare bones contract as long as weight is maintained on or above the line. The potential advantage of this method is that it ensures a reasonably steady weight gain over time. The disadvantage of the method is that it holds back patients who would gain weight more rapidly, perhaps averaging 0.3 kg/day, with the "above previous high weight" contract.

Further refinements of this basic contract are possible. For example, on the first day in which weight is below the contractual level, the patient might be restricted to her room. On the second consecutive day, the patient might be restricted to bed. On the third consecutive day below the contractual level, the patient might be tube fed. This arrangement again makes use of the principle of negative reinforcement, conditions that are aversive enough for the patient to work so as to avoid. Each unit should develop a basic contract that is implemented in almost every case. Within such a basic contract, visiting privileges for family members and friends should be carefully stipulated. Many units do not allow family members to visit during the initial period of weight gain, perhaps the first 3.0 kg to 5.0 kg of weight gain, and visits are usually kept to a minimum, because many patients find such visits upsetting.

The negotiations with the patient center around the extra benefits that may accrue, either from gaining weight more rapidly than the contract stipulates or as various levels of body weight are reached. The choice of such contingencies allows considerable variation in activities, dependent upon the wishes of the individual patient. Contingencies may include time off the unit (at first accompanied and then unaccompanied passes), perhaps at first within the hospital, then on the hospital grounds, and finally off the hospital grounds. Other contingencies might include access to television and reading materials in the patient's room, more frequent visits from friends, access to physical therapy, a trip to a shopping center with a relative, or an overnight pass home. Considerable ingenuity is possible during the elaboration of such bonus contingencies.

Once the outlines of the contract have been negotiated with the patient, the agreement should be written out by the patient and further discussed until it is acceptable to both the patient and the treatment team. The document should then be signed by the patient and therapist. A copy should be placed in the patient's chart, and the original kept by the patient, usually prominently displayed on a wall.

The Weight-Gain Phase. Other aspects of the treatment program contained in the basic contract should be explained to the patient during the negotiation period, but will be described here for the sake of clarity. These include the provision of an adequate number of calories each day and informational feedback concerning progress. The patient's weight is determined at a standard time each day, usually first thing in the morning. The patient will wear only a hospital gown during this weighing. Patients may use various methods to outwit the nursing staff during this process. Some patients will drink water before weighing or will not empty their bladder. Others will secrete lead weights under their gowns. Such tactics are doomed to failure, for it is only possible to inflate one's weight by a few pounds, and if the tactic is forgotten or discovered, the contractual contingencies will come into force. Weight and caloric intake should be plotted by the patient each day on a graph kept prominently displayed in the room.

Patients are served their meals while alone in their rooms during the initial part of this phase. They may select any foods available on the hospital menu, but the dietitian will supplement the foods selected in order to serve at least 4,000 calories daily, as well as to ensure a balanced choice of foodstuffs. Although this amount of food seems to be large, studies have shown that anorexics will eventually need to consume between 3,000 and 4,000 calories each day in order to gain weight. Patients are asked to sit by each meal in their room for 45 minutes, and the tray is served and removed by the nursing staff without comment on the amount eaten. As weight increases, patients may begin to eat in the company of others. Some programs have attempted to reinforce eating behavior by having a member of the treatment team sit with the patient and make conversation contingent upon the patient eating a mouthful of food. This is a somewhat clumsy method to use in practice, and one that has not been demonstrated to be particularly useful, because such eating behaviors are within the patient's repertoire and will be reinforced automatically by the weight-gain contingencies.

Patients may also be asked to count the number of bites of food that they eat and to plot the number for each meal and for each day on a graph. Such a record is useful to the patient because the number of bites taken nicely parallels caloric intake, allowing the patient to better adjust the amount eaten in order to gain the desired amount of weight. Caloric intake is also made available to the patient each day, based on the previous day's consumption. Treatment staff can review this information with the patient, giving appropriate praise for achievements and helping the patient to discern relationships between food intake and weight increases. One of the major advantages of this program is that it helps the anorexic patient to eat three or more meals each day, to choose a wide range of foods, and to spread her or his caloric intake normally over the day. Moreover, behaviors such as self-induced vomiting or excessive exercise tend to be eliminated because they slow down weight gain.

One problem that may arise during the initial phase of weight gain is fluid retention. Patients often react very negatively to the swelling of their legs and arms, confusing fluid with fat. Even more problematic is the subsequent diuresis that may result in a weight loss of one or more kilograms. The best way to handle this problem is to reassure the patient that this is a well-known and temporary problem during weight gain. It is probably wise to prepare the patient for the phenomenon of water retention by warning them that it is likely to happen and that it is time-limited. When diuresis occurs and is confirmed by the medical staff, the previous high weight of the contingency contract may be adjusted downwards to take this into account, because the fluid retention and diuresis are not within the patient's control.

Renegotiation of the patient's contract may be necessary to deal with particular problems encountered with the rate of weight gain. This fine tuning of the program should be initiated either by the patient who is having difficulties with one or other aspect of the contract, or by the staff who perceive problems with the process of weight gain. Usually such changes in the contingencies are aimed at increasing the rate or decreasing the variability of weight gain. These aims can be accomplished by the judicious use of bonus contingencies. It should be remembered that if the contingencies do not achieve their aims, this is not the fault of the patient but of the therapy team. Such failures should be carefully examined, changes in the contingencies negotiated, and their effects carefully observed.

Other therapeutic modalities are used in conjunction with this basic weight-management program. For the nonbulimic anorexic, cyproheptadine should be started at the same time as the weight contract is instituted and the dosage increased to a maximum of 32 mg daily. Such a dose is usually well-tolerated and appears to be safe. For the bulimic anorexic, the use of an antidepressant should be considered, because as we saw in chapter 5, such agents may help the patient to control their binge eating and purging. Although still based upon a handful of studies, the first choice of medication should probably be desipramine, which should be given in a single dose at night, up to a maximum of 200 mg per day. Serum desipramine levels should be obtained and the dosage adjusted so that the level is between 125 and 275 ng/ml.

Supportive psychotherapy should also be offered during the phase of weight gain. Such therapy should be directed first at any problems the patient is encountering with the program. In addition, the therapist should begin to help the patient to challenge irrational cognitions concerning body image and food intake, much as in the bulimia protocol described in the previous chapter. Therapy directed toward normalizing body image can be also be provided by physical therapy. Here the patient may be shown the correct way to exercise so as to maintain a reasonable body shape. In addition, therapists can carry out sessions in which patients view themselves in a mirror or on videotape. Direct feedback of this type appears to help correct patients' impressions of themselves as being fat. Practice at food buying and meal preparation in the context of occupational therapy can also help to overcome distorted notions about the caloric value of certain avoided foods and the fear associated with handling such foods.

As weight gain proceeds, particular areas of behavioral deficit, especially in the ability to communicate directly in an assertive manner, should be addressed. Most programs also include family or couples therapy, usually begun after weight gain is well established. Beginning family therapy at an earlier time risks upsetting the patient before new eating behavior is well-established, with a consequent disruption of weight gain. Although there is no experimental evidence for the efficacy of family therapy in the treatment of anorexia nervosa, family communication problems loom large in anorexia nervosa. Because many patients return home, and still others face separation from the family for the first time, family therapy directed at establishing direct and full communication on important issues can be helpful.

As the weight-gain phase proceeds, it will be necessary for the patient and treatment team to negotiate a final weight to be attained and maintained before discharge. Such a weight should be as close as possible to the patient's ideal weight as indicated on the Metropolitan Life tables (1983), because this allows the patient to experience a normal body size before discharge from hospital. Upon gaining this weight, the maintenance phase begins.

Maintenance Phase. This phase is usually between 7 and 10 days in length. The weight contract should now be changed so that reinforcement is contingent upon maintaining weight with a range of about 0.6 kg above or below the goal. This allows the patient to experience the effects of a more normal caloric intake and a reasonable exercise program. Activities should be restricted as little as possible and trips for job interviews should be encouraged if appropriate. For the bulimic anorexic, this is an ideal time to begin the full bulimia protocol as described in the previous chapter, in preparation for discharge.

Although planning for discharge will have begun during the final days of the weight-gain phase, these plans must not be fine tuned. If the patient is to return home, then brief visits home, at first for the day and then overnight, should be arranged. These visits should be prepared for in the family sessions, and issues such as menus should be fully explored before setting up the visit. If the patient is to return to another environment, then visits of increasing duration to that environment should be set up in a similar manner. Problems encountered during such visits should be fully explored, and solutions to them sought using the problem-solving procedures outlined in chapters 3 and 6.

Finally, planning for follow-up therapy should be completed. This is often difficult for the anorexic patient because, given the rarity of the disorder, patients may live at long distances from the treatment unit. Such units will need to maintain a list of therapists in various areas from which patients are referred. Alternatively, the patient may wish to move to the community in which the unit is located in order to continue with treatment. At this time, a weight below which the patient will be readmitted to the treatment unit should be negotiated with the patient and discussed with the patient's follow-up therapist. Such a weight might be 5 kg below the maintenance goal. The advantage of setting a fairly stringent readmission weight is that retreatment can be considerably shortened if the patient has not lost too much weight before readmission.

Follow-up Therapy. Although restoration of normal body weight can be accomplished in a timely manner in the majority of patients, residual problems such as distortions of body image, restricted food intake, and distorted beliefs about food, as well as social problems such as inadequate interpersonal and job-related skills, are commonplace. Undoubtedly these residual problems predispose toward the relatively high relapse rates encountered in the treatment of anorexia nervosa. Outpatient therapy, then, has two aims: to prevent relapse and to extend the gains of in-hospital treatment.

The first task of the therapist, once outpatient treatment has begun, is to reaffirm the patient's goal weight and to specify the weight criterion for readmission to hospital. It is usually not desirable for patients to weigh themselves each day, because this tends to aggravate their morbid preoccupation with weight. It is preferable that the patient should continue to allow the therapist or nurse to weigh them at each visit. As was the case in hospital, this weight should be plotted on a graph, with the readmission weight clearly drawn across the graph.

Patients should also be asked to monitor their food intake, the circumstances of eating, feelings associated with eating, and particular beliefs about eating, as described for the treatment of bulimia. Should self-induced vomiting, laxative use, or excessive exercise be problems, then these behaviors should also be recorded. This information should form the core data for review and discussion in each therapy session. As described for bulimia, the aim should be for the patient to eat three adequate meals each day. A slow shaping paradigm should be used to accomplish this aim. In addition, feared and avoided foods should be slowly added to these meals. The circumstances of eating should also be carefully examined, because many anorexic individuals do not consume food sitting at a table or using utensils. Again, a slow shaping paradigm should be used to normalize this behavior.

For the bulimic anorexic, the full protocol described in chapter 6 should be implemented, including the use of in-session response prevention. In all cases, one of the core features of therapy consists in identifying and challenging the distorted cognitions associated with body image, with food intake, and with the need for purging. This approach to therapy has been discussed in some detail by a number of workers, particularly Garfinkel and his colleagues (e.g., Garner, Garfinkel, & Bemis, 1982), and will be outlined here.

The first step in dealing with distorted cognitions is to *articulate the beliefs* associated with the various behaviors that the therapist is helping the patient to change. The presence of such beliefs is usually indicated by a failure of the patient to carry through an agreed-upon behavior change. Such failures should lead to a careful exploration of the thinking associated with the particular behavior, so that the belief can be precisely and fully articulated. Once this is done, the therapist should be alert for the repeated circumstances in which this particular distorted belief is demonstrated. Simply clarifying the belief may result in the patient recognizing the distortions involved. In other cases, repeated articulation of the belief, with consistent challenge and the framing of a more rational alternative belief, is needed before behavior changes can occur.

Cognitive imperatives are also frequently used by the anorexic. Many rules governing personal behavior are framed with the words "should" and "must," and reveal the perfectionistic attitudes so common in these patients. Such statements as "I must throw up whenever I eat a sweet food" should be challenged consistently by the therapist, and the patient has to be persuaded to take the risk of not following through on such imperatives. Suggestions to take an experimental view of such new behavior are sometimes successful with the anorexic or bulimic patient. When the behavior has been accomplished, a thorough review of the consequences should be undertaken. The patient is often surprised that not only did no adverse consequence occur, but that the behavior was accompanied by unexpected positive consequences.

Catastrophic thinking is also frequently demonstrated by anorexic patients. Usually, the imagined negative consequences of a particular behavior are much exaggerated. A typical statement might be "Eating a piece of cake will cause me to gain 2 lb in weight"; or "Because I have put on a pound in weight, everyone will think that I'm fat and won't like me any more." In such cases, the reality of the imagined consequences must be carefully examined, based as far as possible on the patient's past experiences, as well as upon the actual realities of the imagined consequences.

Reattribution can also be used, especially in connection with the patient's body image distortions. As well as challenging the reality of beliefs about fatness, the therapist may find it useful to suggest that it is the patient's perception that is at fault, not the reality of her body. In this way patients can be brought to challenge their perceptions.

Follow-up therapy ideally should be continued until the patient has experienced a stable weight for several months and has also demonstrated improvement in interpersonal behavior, work-related behavior, and eating behavior, including the beliefs previously discussed. Given the deficit in social learning that has occurred as a result of missing many normal adolescent socialization experiences, there is probably a limit to the degree to which many anorexics can be rehabilitated. Treatment should continue until the therapist feels that such a limit has been reached. Once active treatment has been concluded, it is important to have the patient attend follow-up visits. In these visits continued progress can be assessed at less frequent intervals, perhaps at first at 3-month intervals, then 6 months, and finally at an annual follow-up visit.

OUTPATIENT TREATMENT

The usual indication for the hospitalization of a patient diagnosed as having anorexia nervosa is a weight loss that is 25% or more of ideal body weight. At this weight, it is extraordinarily difficult for the patient to consume the requisite number of calories needed to gain weight steadily outside of a hospital. Moreover, potentially dangerous medical complications are more probable at such low weights. At a somewhat higher level of weight, perhaps 15 to 20% below ideal body weight, outpatient treatment of the disorder might be considered.

The principles involved in treatment are exactly the same as those outlined for inpatient care and outpatient follow-up. Assessment should be followed by an agreement that unless weight is gained at a reasonable rate (e.g., 0.1 kg/day determined by measurements at weekly intervals) the patient and family will agree to immediate hospitalization. Following this agreement, baseline weight should be determined, and a weight line below which hospital care will begin should be drawn on a graph. Note that a slower rate of weight gain is suggested for an outpatient program as contrasted with an inpatient program.

Treatment should commence by working out a reinforcement system for weight gain, should it be feasible and appropriate. Such a system will probably only be possible for the younger anorexic living at home, although for the college-age patient, return to college at a particular weight level can be reinforcing. For the younger anorexic, privileges and pocket money can be made contingent upon weight gain using a point economy. In addition to contingency management, the other elements of therapy previously outlined should be instituted as appropriate.

The major problem in outpatient treatment is the difficulty that patients have in consuming more than 3,000 calories each day, in addition to making changes in exercise levels, self-induced vomiting, etc. Furthermore, family interactions may complicate the recovery process requiring intervention at the family level. Nonetheless, the weight line will ensure that lack of progress will lead to hospitalization, thus providing a natural endpoint should outpatient therapy not produce the requisite gains in weight.

ED-H

Afterword

The field of therapeutic behavior change has matured in the past 25 years, a development dependent on an increasingly vigorous research effort. No longer will the confident and sometimes dogmatic assertions of experienced clinicians suffice to guide us in the care of our patients. Instead, the research literature should be the basis for choosing our therapeutic strategies. This approach is reflected in the pages of this book, in which the latest developments in therapeutic research have been transformed into practical treatment procedures for the three major eating disorders: obesity, bulimia, and anorexia nervosa.

Although the research efforts of the past 25 years have resulted in steady improvements in our ability to effectively treat patients with one or other of the eating disorders, it is also true that much remains to be done. Thus, although the treatment procedures outlined in this book are "modern" in the sense that they reflect the current status of research in the field, it is hoped that they will be improved upon as new research findings become available. Although authors might like their books on treatment to last, our patients should hope that they rapidly become outmoded!

References

Adams, N., Ferguson, J., Stunkard, A. J., & Agras, W. S. (1978). The eating behavior of obese and nonobese women. *Behaviour Research and Therapy, 16,* 225–232.

Agras, W. S., & Arnow, B. (in press). Behavioral treatment of obesity. In P. V. J. Beumont, G. D. Burrows, & R. Casper (Eds.), *Handbook of eating disorders: Volume 2. Obesity.* Amsterdam: Elsevier.

Agras, W. S., Barlow, D. H., Chapin, H. N., Abel, G. G., & Leitenberg, H. (1974). Behavior modification of anorexia nervosa. *Archives of General Psychiatry, 30,* 279–286.

Agras, W. S., Dorian, B., Kirkley, B. G., Arnow, B., & Bachman, J. (in press) Imipramine in the treatment of bulimia: A double-blind controlled study. *International Journal of Eating Disorders.*

Agras, W. S., & Kirkley, B. G. (1986). Bulimia: Theories of etiology. In K. D. Brownell & J. P. Foreyt (Eds.), *Handbook of eating disorders: Physiology, psychology, and treatment of obesity, anorexia, and bulimia* (pp. 365–378). New York: Basic Books.

Agras, W. S., & Kraemer, H. C. (1983). The treatment of anorexia nervosa: Do different treatments have different outcomes? In A. J. Stunkard & E. Stellor (Eds.), *Eating and its disorders* (pp. 286–302). New York: Raven.

American Psychiatric Association. (1980). *Diagnostic and statistical manual of mental disorders* (3rd Ed.). Washington, DC: American Psychiatric Association.

Bachrach, A. J., Erwin, W. J., & Mohr, J. P. (1965). The control of eating behavior in an anorexic by operant conditioning techniques. In L. P. Ullman & L. Krasner (Eds.), *Case studies in behavior modification* (pp. 153–163). New York: Holt, Rhinehart, & Winston.

Bandura, A. (1977). *Social learning theory.* Englewood Cliffs, NJ: Prentice-Hall.

Beck, A. T. (1976). *Cognitive therapy and the emotional disorders.* New York: International Universities Press.

Beck, A. T., Ward, C., Mendelsohn, M., Mock, M., & Erbaugh, J. (1961). An inventory for measuring depression. *Archives of General Psychiatry, 120,* 561–571.

Berkowitz, R. I., Agras, W. S., Korner, A. F., Kraemer, H. C., & Zeanah, C. H. (1985). Physical activity and adiposity: A longitudinal study from birth to childhood. *Journal of Pediatrics, 106,* 734–741.

Blair, S. N., Clark, D. G., & Kohl, H. W. (1986). *Physical activity and prevention of obesity in childhood.* Position paper presented at NICHD Workshop on Childhood Obesity, Bethesda, Maryland.

Blinder, B. J., Freeman, D. M. A., & Stunkard, A. J. (1970). Behavior therapy of anorexia nervosa: Effectiveness of activity as a reinforcer of weight gain. *American Journal of Psychiatry, 126,* 77–82.

Brotman, A. W., Herzog, D. B., & Woods, S. W. (1984). Antidepressant treatment of bulimia: The relationship between bingeing and depressive symptomatology. *Journal of Clinical Psychiatry, 45,* 7–9.

107

Brownell, K. D., Heckerman, C. L., Westlake, R. J., Hayes, S. C., & Monti, P. M. (1978). The effect of couples' training and partner co-operativeness in the behavioral treatment of obesity. *Behaviour Research & Therapy, 16,* 323–333.

Brownell, K. D., & Stunkard, A. J. (1978). Behavior therapy and behavior change: Uncertainties in programs for weight control. *Behaviour Research & Therapy, 16,* 323–325.

Brownell, K. D., & Stunkard, A. J. (1981). Differential changes in plasma high-density-lipoprotein cholesterol levels in obese men and women during weight reduction. *Archives of Internal Medicine, 141,* 1142–1146.

Brownell, K. D., & Wadden, T. A. (1986). Behavior therapy for obesity: Modern approaches and better results. In K. D. Brownell & J. P. Foreyt (Eds.), *Handbook of eating disorders: Physiology, psychology, and treatment of obesity, anorexia, and bulimia* (pp. 180–197). New York: Basic Books.

Bureau of the Census. (1983). *Statistical abstract of the United States* (pp. 103–126). Washington, DC: Author.

Burnett, K. F., Taylor, C. B., & Agras, W. S. (1985). Ambulatory computer-assisted therapy for obesity: A new frontier for behavior therapy. *Journal of Consulting & Clinical Psychology, 53,* 698–703.

Cabanac, M., & Duclaux, R. (1970). Obesity: Absence of satiety aversion to sucrose. *Science, 168,* 496–497.

Cooper, P. J., & Fairburn, C. G. (1983). Binge eating and self-induced vomiting in the community. *British Journal of Psychiatry, 142,* 139–144.

Craighead, L. W. (1984). Sequencing of behavior therapy and pharmacotherapy for obesity. *Journal of Consulting and Clinical Psychology, 52,* 190–199.

Craighead, L. W., Stunkard, A. J., & O'Brien, R. (1981). Behavior therapy and pharmacotherapy of obesity. *Archives of General Psychiatry, 38,* 763–768.

Crisp, A. H. (1983). Treatment and outcome in anorexia nervosa. In R. K. Goldstein (Ed.), *Eating and weight disorders* (pp. 91–104). New York: Springer.

Crisp, A. H., Hall, A., & Holland, A. J. (1985). Nature and nurture in anorexia nervosa. A study of 34 pairs of twins, 1 pair of triplets, and an adoptive family. *International Journal of Eating Disorders, 4,* 5–28.

Crisp, A. H., Palmer, R. L., & Kalucy, R. S. (1976). How common is anorexia nervosa? A prevalence study. *British Journal of Psychiatry, 218,* 549–554.

Dine, M. S., Gartside, P. S., Glueck, C., Rheines, L., Greene, G., & Khoury, P. (1979). Where do the heaviest children come from? A prospective study of white children from birth to 5 years of age. *Pediatrics, 63,* 1–7.

Drabman, R. S., Cordua, G., Hammer, D., Jarvie, G. J., & Horton, W. (1979). Developmental trends in eating rates of normal and overweight preschool children. *Child Development, 50,* 211–216.

Dubbert, P., & Wilson, G. T. (1983). Treatment failures in behavior therapy for obesity: Causes, correlations, and consequences. In E. Foa & P. M. G. Emmelkamp (Eds.), *Treatment failure in behavior therapy* (pp. 107–131). New York: Wiley.

Dubbert, P., & Wilson, G. T. (in press). Goal setting and spouse involvement in the treatment of obesity. *Behaviour Research and Therapy.*

Dwyer, J. T., Feldman, J. J., Seltzer, C. C., & Mayer, J. (1969). Body image in adolescents: Attitudes towards weight and perception of appearance. *American Journal of Clinical Nutrition, 20,* 1045–1056.

Eckert, E. D., Goldberg, S. C., Casper, R. C., & Halmi, K. A. (1979). Cyproheptadine in anorexia nervosa. *British Journal of Psychiatry, 134,* 67–70.

Elkin, T. E., Hersen, M., Eisler, R. M., & Williams, J. G. (1973). Modification of caloric intake in anorexia nervosa: An experimental analysis. *Psychological Reports, 32,* 75–78.

Fairburn, C. G. (1981). A cognitive–behavioral approach to the treatment of bulimia. *Psychological Medicine, 11,* 707–711.

Fairburn, C. G., & Garner, D. M. (1986). The diagnosis of bulimia nervosa. *International Journal of Eating Disorders, 5,* 403-420.

Ferguson, J. M., Marquis, J. N., & Taylor, C. B. (1977). A script for deep muscle relaxation. *Diseases of the Nervous System, 38,* 703-708.

Ferster, L. B., Nurnberger, J. L., & Levitt, E. B. (1962). The control of eating. *Journal of Mathetics, 1,* 87-109.

Follick, M. J., Abrams, D. B., Smith, T. W., Henderson, L. O., & Herbert, P. N. (1984). Contrasting short- and long-term effects of weight loss on lipoprotein levels. *Archives of Internal Medicine, 144,* 1571-1574.

Fomon, S. J., Rogers, R., Ziegler, E. E., Nelson, S. E., & Thomas, L. N. (1984). Indices of fatness and serum cholesterol at age 8 years in relation to feeding and growth during early infancy. *Pediatric Research, 18,* 1233-1238.

Frank, A., Graham, C., & Frank, S. (1981). Fatalities on the liquid-protein diet: An analysis of possible causes. *International Journal of Obesity, 5,* 243-248.

Freedman, D. S., Burke, G. L., Harsha, D. W., Srinivasan, S. R., Cresanta, J. L., Webber, L. S., & Berenson, G. S. (1985). Relationship of changes in obesity to serum lipid and lipoprotein changes in childhood and adolescence. *Journal of the American Medical Association, 254,* 515-520.

Gambrill, E. D., & Richey, C. A. (1975). An assertion inventory for use in assessment and research. *Behaviour Research & Therapy, 6,* 550-561.

Garner, D. M., & Garfinkel, P. E., (1979). The Eating Attitude Test: An index of the symptoms of anorexia nervosa. *Psychological Medicine, 9,* 273-279.

Garner, D. M., Garfinkel, P. E., & Bemis, K. M. (1982). A multidimensional psychotherapy for anorexia nervosa. *International Journal of Eating Disorders, 1,* 3-46.

Garner, D. M., Garfinkel, P. E., Schwartz, D., & Thompson, M. (1980). Cultural expectation of thinness in women. *Psychological Reports, 47,* 483-491.

Giles, T. R., Young, R. R., & Young, D. E. (1985). Behavioral treatment of severe bulimia. *Behavior Therapy, 16,* 393-405.

Graham, L. E., Taylor, C. B., Hovell, M. F., & Siegel, W. (1983). Five-year follow-up to a behavioral weight-loss program. *Journal of Consulting and Clinical Psychology, 51,* 321-323.

Gross, H. A., Ebert, M. H., & Faden, V. V. (1981). A double-blind controlled trial of lithium carbonate in primary anorexia nervosa. *Journal of Clinical Psychopharmacology, 1,* 376-381.

Halmi, K. A., Eckert, E., LaDu, T. J., & Cohen, J. (1986). Anorexia nervosa: Treatment efficacy of cyproheptadine and amitriptyline. *Archives of General Psychiatry, 43,* 177-181.

Herman, C. P., & Mack, D. (1975). Restrained and unrestrained eating. *Journal of Personality, 43,* 647-660.

Hsu, L. K. G. (1980). Outcome of anorexia nervosa: A review of the literature (1954 to 1978). *Archives of General Psychiatry, 37,* 1041-1043.

Hudson, J. I., Laffer, P. S., & Pope, H. G. (1982). Bulimia related to affective disorder by family history and response to the dexamethasone suppression test. *American Journal of Psychiatry, 139,* 685-687.

Hughes, P. L., Wells, L. A., Cunningham, C. J., & Ilstrup, D. M. (1986). Treating bulimia with desipramine: A double-blind, placebo-controlled study. *Archives of General Psychiatry, 43,* 182-186.

Isner, J. M., Sours, H. E., Paris, A. L., Farrans, V. J., & Roberts, W. C. (1979). Sudden unexpected death in avid dieters using the liquid protein modified fast diet. *Circulation, 60,* 1401-1412.

Jacobs, M. B., & Schneider, J. A. (1985). Medical complications of bulimia: A prospective evaluation. *Quarterly Journal of Medicine, 54,* 177-182.

Jeffery, R. W., Björnson-Benson, W. M., Rosenthal, B. S., Kurth, C. L., & Dunn, M. M. (1984). Effectiveness of monetary contracts with two repayment schedules on weight reduction in men and women from self-referred and population samples. *Behavior Therapy, 15,* 273-279.

Johnson, W. G., Wildman, H. E., & O'Brien, T. (1980). The assessment of program adherence: The

Achilles heel of behavioral weight reduction? *Behavioral Assessment, 2,* 297-301.

Jonas, J. M., Hudson, J. I., & Pope, H. G. (1983). Treatment of bulimia with MAO inhibitors. *Journal of Clinical Psychopharmacology, 3,* 59-60.

Keefe, P. H., Wyshogrod, D., Weinberger, E., & Agras, W. S. (1984). Binge eating and outcome of behavioral treatment of obesity: A preliminary report. *Behaviour Reserach & Therapy, 22,* 319-321.

Kirkley, B. G., Agras, W. S., & Weiss, J. J. (1985). Nutritional inadequacy in the diets of treated bulimics. *Behavior Therapy, 16,* 287-291.

Kirkley, B. G., Schneider, J. A., Agras, W. S., & Bachman, J. A. (1985). Comparison of two group-treatments for bulimia. *Journal of Consulting and Clinical Psychology, 53,* 43-48.

Kramer, M. S., Barr, R. G., Leduc, G., Boisjoly, C., McVey-White, L., & Pless, B. (1985). *Journal of Pediatrics, 106,* 10-14.

Lacey, J. H. (1983). Bulimia nervosa, binge eating, and psychogenic vomiting: A controlled treatment study and long-term outcome. *British Journal of Psychiatry, 286,* 1609-1612.

Lacey, J. H., & Crisp, A. H. (1980). Hunger, food intake, and weight. The impact of clomipramine on a refeeding anorexia nervosa population. *Postgraduate Medical Journal, 56,* 79-85.

Lansky, D. (1978). A methodological analysis of research on adherence and weight loss. Reply to Brownell & Stunkard, 1978. *Behavior Therapy, 12,* 144-149.

Lee, N. L., & Rush, A. J. (1986). Cognitive-behavioral group therapy for bulimia. *International Journal of Eating Disorders, 5,* 599-615.

Leitenberg, H., Agras, W. S., Edwards, J. A., & Thompson, L. E. (1970). Practice as a psychotherapeutic variable: An experimental analysis within single cases. *Journal of Psychiatric Research, 7,* 215-225.

Leitenberg, H., Gross, J., Peterson, J., & Rosen, J. C. (1984). Analysis of an anxiety model and the process of change during exposure and response prevention treatment of bulimia nervosa. *Behavior Therapy, 15,* 1-20.

Linn, R., & Stuart, S. L. (1976). *The last chance diet.* Newark, NJ: Lyle Stuart.

Luka, L. P., Agras, W. S., & Schneider, J. A., (1986). Thirty-month follow-up of cognitive-behavioral group therapy for bulimia. *British Journal of Psychiatry, 148,* 614-615.

MacMahon, S. W., Wilcken, D. E. L., & Macdonald, J. (1986). The effect of weight reduction on left ventricular mass: A randomized controlled trial in young, overweight, hypertensive patients. *New England Journal of Medicine, 314,* 334-340.

Metropolitan Life Insurance Company. (1983). *Metropolitan height and weight tables.* New York: Society of Actuaries and Association of Life Insurance Medical Directors.

Mills, H. L., Agras, W. S., Barlow, D. H., Baugh, J. R. & Mills, J. R. (1973). The treatment of compulsive rituals by response prevention: A sequential analysis of treatment variables. *Archives of General Psychiatry, 28,* 569-576.

Mitchell, J. E., & Groat, R. (1984). A placebo-controlled, double-blind trial of amitriptyline in bulimia. *Journal of Clinical Psychopharmacology, 4,* 186-193.

Mook, D. G., & Cseh, C. L. (1981). Release of feeding by the sweet taste in rats: The influence of body weight. *Appetite, 2,* 15-34.

National Institutes of Health Consensus Development Conference Statement. (1985). Health implications of obesity. *Annals of Internal Medicine, 103,* 1073-1077.

Nutzinger, D. O., Cayiroglu, S., Sachs, G., & Zapotoczky, H. G. (1985). Emotional problems during weight reduction: Advantages of a combined behavior therapy and antidepressive drug therapy for obesity. *Journal of Behavior Therapy and Experimental Psychiatry, 16,* 217-222.

Nylander, I. (1971). The feeling of being fat and dieting in a school population: Epidemiologic, interview investigation. *Acta Sociomedical Scandinavica, 3,* 17-26.

Ordman, A. M., & Kirschenbaum, D. S. (1985). Cognitive-behavioral therapy for bulimia: An initial outcome study. *Journal of Consulting and Clinical Psychology, 53,* 305-313.

Paffenberger, R. S., Hyde, R. T., Wing, A. L., & Hsieh, C. (1986). Physical activity, all-cause mortality, and longevity of college alumni. *New England Journal of Medicine, 314,* 605–613.

Pillay, M., & Crisp, A. H. (1981). The impact of social-skills training within an established inpatient treatment program for anorexia nervosa. *British Journal of Psychiatry, 139,* 533–539.

Pope, H. G., & Hudson, J. I., (1982). Treatment of bulimia with antidepressants. *Psychopharmacology, 78,* 176–179.

Pope, H. G., Hudson, J. I., Jonas, J. M., & Yurgelun-Todd, D. (1983). Bulimia treated with imipramine: A placebo-controlled, double-blind study. *American Journal of Psychiatry, 140,* 554–558.

Pyle, R. L., Halvorson, A., Neuman, P. A., & Mitchell, J. E. (1986). The increasing prevalence of bulimia in freshman college students. *International Journal of Eating Disorders, 5,* 631–648.

Reisin, E., Abel, R., Modan, M., Silverberg, D. S., Eliahou, H., & Modan, B. (1978). Effect of weight loss without salt-restriction on the reduction of blood pressure in overweight hypertensive patients. *New England Journal of Medicine, 298,* 1–5.

Rodin, J., Slochower, J., & Fleming, B. (1977). The effects of degree of obesity, age of onset, and energy deficit on external responsiveness. *Journal of Comparative Physiology and Psychology, 91,* 586–597.

Rodin, J., Slochower, J., & Fleming, B. (1977). The effects of degree of obesity, age of onset, and energy deficit on external responsiveness. *Journal of Comparative Physiology and Psychology, 91,* 586–597.

Rosenthal, T. L., & Downs, A. (1985). Cognitive aids in teaching and treating. *Advances in Behaviour Therapy & Research, 7,* 1–53.

Schneider, J. A., & Agras, W. S. (1985). A cognitive–behavioral group treatment of bulimia. *British Journal of Psychiatry, 146,* 66–69.

Smith, P. L., Gold, A. R., Meyers, D. A., Haponik, E. F., & Bleecker, E. R. (1985). Weight loss in mildly to moderately obese patients with obstructive sleep apnea. *Annals of Internal Medicine, 103,* 850–855.

Smith, U. (1985). Regional differences in adipocyte metabolism and possible consequences in vivo. *International Journal of Obesity, 9,* 145–148.

Sorile, P., Gordon, T., & Kannel, W. B. (1980). Body build and mortality. *Journal of the American Medical Association, 243,* 1828–1831.

Stalonas, P. M., & Kirschenbaum, D. S. (1985). Behavioral treatments for obesity: Eating habits revisited. *Behavior Therapy, 19,* 1–14.

Stangler, R. S., & Printz, A. M. (1980). *DSM-III:* Psychiatry diagnosis in a university population. *American Journal of Psychiatry, 137,* 937–940.

Stewart, J. W., Walsh, B. T., Wright, L., Roose, S. P., & Glassman, A. H. (1984). An open trial of MAO inhibitors in bulimia. *Journal of Clinical Psychiatry, 45,* 217–219.

Stunkard, A. J., Coll., S. L., Lundquist, S., & Meyers, A. (1980). Obesity and eating style. *Archives of General Psychiatry, 37,* 1127–1129.

Stunkard, A. J., D'Aquili, E., Fox, S., & Filion, R. D. (1972). Influence of social class on obesity and thinness in children. *Journal of the American Medical Association, 221,* 579–584.

Stunkard, A. J., & Kaplan, P. (1977). Eating in public places: A review of reports on the direct observations of eating behavior. *International Journal of Obesity, 1,* 89–101.

Stunkard, A. J., Sorenson, T. I. A., Hanis, C., Teasdale, T. W., Chakraborty, R., Schull, W. J., & Schulsinger, F. (1986). An adoption study of human obesity. *New England Journal of Medicine, 314,* 193–198.

Wadden, T. A., & Stunkard, A. J. (1986). Controlled trial of very-low-calorie diet, behavior therapy, and their combination in the treatment of obesity. *Journal of Consulting and Clinical Psychology, 54,* 482–486.

Walsh, B. T., Stewart, J. W., Roose, S. P., Gladis, M., & Glassman, A. H. (1984). Treatment of bulimia with phenelzine: A double-blind placebo-controlled study. *Archives of General Psychiatry, 43,* 1105–1109.

Willi, J., & Grossman, S. (1983). Epidemiology of anorexia nervosa in a defined region of Switzerland. *American Journal of Psychiatry, 140,* 564–567.

Wilson, G. T. (1980). Behavior therapy for obesity. *Advances in Behavior Research and Therapy, 3,* 49–83.

Wilson, G. T. (1985). Psychological prognostic factors in the treatment of obesity. In J. Hirsch & T. Van Itallie (Eds.), *Recent advances in obesity research, Vol. 4.* London: John Libbey & Co.

Wilson, G. T., Rossiter, E., Kleifield, E. I., & Lindholm, L. (1986). Cognitive–behavioral treatment of bulimia nervosa: A controlled evaluation. *Behaviour Research & Therapy, 24,* 277–288.

Wing, R. R., Epstein, L. H., Nowalk, M. P., Koeske, R., & Hagg, S. (in press). Behavior change, weight loss, and physiological improvements in Type II diabetic patients. *Journal of Consulting and Clinical Psychology.*

Wolchik, S. A., Weiss, L., & Katzman, M. A. (1986). An empirically validated, short-term psychoeducational group-treatment program for bulimia. *International Journal of Eating Disorders, 5,* 21–34.

Wurtman, J., Wurtman, R., Mark, S., Tsay, R., Gilbert, R., & Growdon, J. (1985). d-Fenfluramine selectively suppresses carbohydrate snacking by obese subjects. *International Journal of Eating Disorders, 4,* 89–100.

Wyshogrod, D. (1985). Current treatment of obesity exemplified in a case study. *Journal of Behavior Therapy and Experimental Psychiatry, 16,* 151–157.

Appendix A.
Stanford Eating
Disorders Questionnaire

Name: _____ Sex: M F Age: ___ Birthdate: _____

Address: _____ Home phone: (___)_____

_____ Work phone: (___)_____

Zip Code

1. Describe your present occupation: _____

_____

2. How long have you worked for your present employer? _____

3. Circle the last year of school attended:

Grade School	High School	College		
1 2 3 4 5 6 7 8	9 10 11 12	1 2 3 4	MA	PhD

4. Present marital status (circle one):   Single   married   divorced
                                            separated   engaged

5. Answer the following questions about each marriage:

Dates of marriage	Dates of termination	Reason (death, divorce)	Number of children
_____	_____	_____	_____
_____	_____	_____	_____
_____	_____	_____	_____

6. Spouse's age: _____   Weight: _____   Height: _____

7. Spouse's occupation: _____

8. Describe your spouse's weight (circle one):

| Very overweight | Slightly overweight | About average | Slightly underweight | Very underweight |

9. List your children's ages, sex, height, and weights and check off whether they are overweight, average, or underweight. Include any children from previous marriages, whether they are living with you or not.

				Overweight		Underweight
Age	Sex	Weight	Height	Very / Slight	Average	Slight / Very
___	___	___	___	___ ___	___	___ ___
___	___	___	___	___ ___	___	___ ___
___	___	___	___	___ ___	___	___ ___
___	___	___	___	___ ___	___	___ ___
___	___	___	___	___ ___	___	___ ___

10. Who lives at home with you? _____

WEIGHT HISTORY

11. Your present weight: _____   Height: _____

12. Describe your present weight (circle one):

| Very overweight | Slightly overweight | About average |

13. How much would you really like to weigh? _____

14. How do you feel about the way you <u>look</u> at your present weight? (circle one)

| Completely Satisfied | Satisfied | Neutral | Dissatisfied | Very Dissatisfied |

15. How does your present weight affect your daily activities? (circle one)

| No effect | Some effect | Often interferes | Extreme effect |

Describe: _____

_____

16. What are the attitudes of the following people about your weight?

	Negative (They disapprove)	Indifferent	Positive (They like you at this weight)
Spouse	_____	_____	_____
Children	_____	_____	_____
Parents	_____	_____	_____
Employer	_____	_____	_____
Friends (include roommates)	_____	_____	_____

17. Do these attitudes affect your weight loss or gain?   Yes   No

    If yes, explain: _____

    _____

    _____

    _____

18. On the table on p. 116, indicate the periods in your life when you have been overweight or underweight. List your weight for each period and the number of pounds you were under-/overweight. Describe any methods you used to lose weight, drawing from the list at the bottom of the table. For each such method, indicate how many pounds you lost and over what length of time. Also list any significant life events you feel were related to either your weight loss or gain, e.g., college tests, marriage, pregnancies, illness.

19. Which types of food are particularly troublesome/tempting (e.g., sweets, starches)?

    _____

    _____

20. Do you ever feel that your eating pattern is abnormal or unusual compared to other people, either in amount eaten or rate of eating?

    Yes   No   Don't know

21. Do you ever eat large amounts of food very quickly in a short amount of time?

    Yes   No   Don't know

Age	Weight	Pounds Over-Weight	Pounds Under-Weight	Methods Used to Lose/Gain Weight	Pounds Lost(-)/ Gained(+)	Duration of Attempt	Significant Events Related to Weight Change
Birth	____	____	____	_____	____	____	____
0–5	____	____	____	_____	____	____	____
6–10	____	____	____	_____	____	____	____
11–15	____	____	____	_____	____	____	____
16–20	____	____	____	_____	____	____	____
21–25	____	____	____	_____	____	____	____
26–30	____	____	____	_____	____	____	____
31–35	____	____	____	_____	____	____	____
36–40	____	____	____	_____	____	____	____
41–45	____	____	____	_____	____	____	____
46–50	____	____	____	_____	____	____	____
51–55	____	____	____	_____	____	____	____
56–60	____	____	____	_____	____	____	____
61–65	____	____	____	_____	____	____	____

Methods of weight loss: TOPS, Thin Within, Weight Watchers, NutriSystems, HCG shots, pills, supervised diet, unsupervised diet, starvation, behavior modification, psychotherapy, hypnosis, vomiting, other (describe).

22. Did you ever have episodes of overeating that you would refer to as binges?

        Yes   No   Don't know

23. If you answered "Yes" to question 22, please answer questions 23a, b, and c. If you answered "No" to question 22, please proceed to question 24.

    a. What kind of food would you generally eat in one of these episodes?

        _____

        _____

    b. How much of this food would you eat in an episode of overeating? (e.g., 1 dz donuts, 1 lb of deli meat, etc.)

        _____

        _____

c. How frequently do episodes like this tend to occur?
    (e.g., per week? month? year?)

_____

_____

24. Do you ever eat large quantities of food deliberately out of the sight of other people?

    Yes   No   Don't know

25. Does eating certain kinds of food make you uneasy or anxious?

    Yes   No   Don't know

26. Do you ever *plan* bouts of overeating?

    Yes   No   Don't know

27. Do you ever eat large amounts of food and stop only because of:

    a. abdominal or stomach pain?   Yes   No
    b. interruption by somebody?   Yes   No
    c. going to sleep?   Yes   No

28. Do you ever try to lose weight by:

    a. making yourself vomit?   Yes   No
    b. using water pills (diuretics)? Yes   No
    c. using laxatives?   Yes   No
    d. going on very restrictive diets? Yes   No
    e. strenuous exercise?   Yes   No
    f. fasting?   Yes   No

29. What was your lowest weight since adolescence?   _____ lb

30. What height were you at the time?   _____ inches

31. What was the most weight (in pounds) that you ever *lost in a month*?

    0–2 lb   2.1–5 lb   5.1–10 lb   10.1 + lb

32. What has been your greatest weight *gain in a week*?

    0–2 lb   2.1–5 lb   5.1–10 lb   10.1 + lb

33. How much does your weight fluctuate in a typical *week*?

    0–2 lb   2.1–5 lb   5.1–10 lb   10.1 + lb

34. Do you ever feel out of control while you are eating or have the fear that you won't be able to stop eating?

    Yes   No   Don't know

35. Do you ever feel ashamed, guilty, blue, or disgusted with yourself after eating a large amount of food?

           Yes   No   Don't know

36. How much alcohol do you usually drink per week?

     Beer (oz.) _____

     Wine (glasses) _____

     Hard liquor (oz.) _____

37. How physically active are you?

Very Active	Active	Average	Inactive	Very Inactive
_____	_____	_____	_____	_____

38. What do you do for physical activity, how often, and for how long at a time?

Activity (e.g., swimming, jogging, dancing)	Frequency (daily, weekly, monthly)	Duration (how many minutes, hours)
_____	_____	_____
_____	_____	_____
_____	_____	_____

MEDICAL HISTORY

39. When did you last have a complete physical examination? _____

40. Who is your current doctor? Name: _____

     Address: _____ Phone: _____

41. What medical problems do you have at the present time? _____
_____

42. What medications or drugs do you take regularly and for what?

Medication	Reason For Taking It
_____	_____
_____	_____
_____	_____
_____	_____

43. List any medications, drugs, or foods you are allergic to: _____
_____

44. List any hospitalizations or operations. Indicate your age at each hospital admission.

    Age   Reason For Hospitalization

    _____   _____

    _____   _____

    _____   _____

45. List any serious illnesses you have had that have *not required hospitalization*. Indicate how old you were during each illness.

    Age   Illness

    _____   _____

    _____   _____

    _____   _____

46. Describe any of your medical problems that are complicated by your weight.

    _____

    _____

47. List any psychiatric contact, individual or marital counseling you have had or are now having.

    Age   Reason For Contact   Type of Therapy
                                             (how often seen, by whom)

    _____   _____   _____

    _____   _____   _____

    _____   _____   _____

FAMILY HISTORY

48. Is your father living?   Yes Age: _____
                              No   Age at, and cause of, death: _____
                              Occupation: _____

49. Is your mother living?   Yes Age: _____
                              No   Age at, and cause of, death: _____
                              Occupation: _____

50. Describe your parent's weights *while you were growing up*:
    (check off one for each)

	Very Overweight	Slightly Overweight	About Average	Slightly Underweight	Very Underweight
Father:	_____	_____	_____	_____	_____
Mother:	_____	_____	_____	_____	_____

51. List your brothers' and sisters' age, sex, present weights, heights, and check off whether they are overweight, average, or underweight.

				Overweight			Underweight	
Age	Sex	Weight	Height	Very /	Slight	Average	Slight /	Very
___	__	____	____	____	____	____	____	___
___	__	____	____	____	____	____	____	___
___	__	____	____	____	____	____	____	___
___	__	____	____	____	____	____	____	___

52. Please add any additional information you feel may be relevant to your weight problem. This includes interactions with your family and friends that might sabotage a treatment program, and any additional family or social history that you feel might help us understand your weight problem.

_____

_____

Appendix B.
Problem-Solving Checklist
for Weight Loss

1. Identify Problem
Use food/activity logs to determine problem areas in:

Exercise

	Present		Period
insufficient duration:	_____	mins/session:	_____
insufficient frequency:	_____	sessions/wk:	_____
insufficient intensity:	_____	sustained hr:	_____

insufficient unstructured activity _____

poor or no scheduling of exercise sessions _____

low priority given to exercise _____

other: _____

Eating Behaviors

eating too fast _____

taking large portions _____

always emptying plate or finishing leftovers _____

impulsive eating: _____

irregular eating habits: times _____ place _____

poor food planning (no low-calorie foods available):

   at home _____ at work _____ other

excessive snacking _____

excessive food deprivation _____

eating when not hungry _____

other: _____

Food Choices

nutritionally unbalanced meals _____

too many fats: problem foods: _____

too much sugar: problem foods: _____

sodium/alcohol/caffeine control: _____
insufficient complex carbohydrates and fibers: _____
other high caloric density or problematic foods: _____

Environmental Influences
problematic eating locations/situations (e.g., parties, at work, vacations):
_____
activities concurrent with eating: _____
problematic social influences: _____
too easy access to high-calorie foods: _____
portion sizes too large _____
other: _____

Cognitive Ecology
Fat thoughts (dysfunctional thinking) in the area(s) of:
pounds lost: _____
capabilities: _____
excuses: _____
standards: _____
food thoughts: _____
eating for self-nurturance (e.g., when under stress, tired, overcommitted, etc.): _____
mixed feelings about reaching desired weight: _____

2. **Devise Intervention**

Carefully *analyze the data* (food/activity logs and Problem-Solving Checklist) to determine the problem area to be worked on first.

Brainstorm possible solutions. Reread materials and investigate possibilities further if appropriate. Be creative!

Set reasonable steps to the goal. Setting realistic self-expectations enhances your ability to accurately predict your progress, ultimately maximizing personal power and success.

Schedule time for work on the problem.

Formulate an evaluation/monitoring plan. (Specify how you will know if you have accomplished a goal or subgoal?) Use food/activity logs.

Devise a reward system. Plan nonfood rewards for successful subgoal attainment.

3. **Implement/Evaluate/Revise**

If your intervention meets your expectations, continue on course. Be sure to reward yourself on a regular basis for progress toward your goals.

If your progress is below your expectations after a sustained high-priority effort, ask yourself:

Was the problem dimension identified correctly? If unsure, return to Step 1.

Were reasonable sub-goals specified? Smaller steps to the goal may be indicated.

Remember: You are doing personal research. You may not find the most appropriate course of action on the first attempt. If you have a problem, re-enter the Problem-Solving Checklist as appropriate, and be sure to address each item in the Devise Intervention section for your next experiment.

If, after several good attempts, problems persist, you may want to consider outside input from the workshop leader, a maintenance group, or other resources.

Appendix C.
Instructions for
Deep Muscle Relaxation

The relaxation skills you are learning should be practiced daily, using the tape provided, for 15 to 20 minutes each session. You may practice right after getting up in the morning, but you should not do it the last thing before bed, as you might fall asleep during the procedures themselves. If you would like to practice relaxation just prior to going to sleep and have difficulty remaining awake, simply practice in a sitting position in a straight-backed chair or in some other comfortable chair in which you must sit erect. The benefits of relaxing are gained when you are in a state of passive consciousness. Try to practice the relaxation exercises at times when you are likely to lose control; for example, after binge eating but before purging. At such times, the relaxation can counteract the anxiety leading to purging.

The following points may be helpful to guide you through the deep muscle relaxation procedures:

1. Practice in a quiet environment that is darkened to avoid extraneous sensory stimulation.
2. Practice in a comfortable overstuffed chair with a footrest, or in a recliner. If you must practice relaxation in bed, prop several pillows behind your back so that your body maintains an erect sitting position.
3. Concentration is important. Keep a pad handy so that you can write down chores and other thoughts before relaxation. In this way you can give more complete attention to relaxation itself, rather than focusing your awareness on other matters.
4. Arrange to unplug the telephone; turn down the volume of televisions, radios, stereos; and turn off noisy appliances.
5. Remember that by quickly tensing and then suddenly releasing tension in each muscle group you are inducing a state of rebound relaxation. You do not need to force your muscles to relax. By carrying out the relaxation strat-

egies with immediate tensing and rapid releasing of the tension, you will passively obtain a deeply relaxed state.

6. Focus your awareness on the sensations in your muscles as you tense and release tension in each muscle group sequentially. Take particular note of the different sensations accompanying tension and relaxation. By carefully attending to these sensations, you will become better able to discern variations in your own level of tension, and you will be able to detect the occurrence of tension at lower levels than you have been aware of previously.

7. Go through two tension–release cycles for each muscle group. If a muscle group is not relaxed after two tension release cycles, simply focus your awareness on the muscles in that group for an additional 30–45 seconds and go through an additional tension–release cycle. Two or three such cycles are usually sufficient for any muscle group. However, it is perfectly okay for you to use as many cycles as you like in order to relax a muscle group.

8. Tense the muscles in any group for 5–7 seconds, allowing them to relax for 30–45 seconds after each tensing.

9. There is no need to produce a great deal of tension in a particular muscle group. Tensing a muscle group as tightly as you can may, in fact, interfere with relaxation. You should tense the muscles of the feet about half as tightly as the muscles of the other groups.

10. Always practice with your eyes closed. Remove watches, contact lenses, belts, or restrictive clothing such as shoes.

11. When tensing a muscle group, attempt to keep the involvement of adjacent muscles to a minimum. There is value in keeping a muscle group still after you have relaxed it.

The 14 muscle groups that we will be using initially are listed below. After each group is a brief description of the most common tensing strategy for the muscles in that group.

1. Dominant hand and forearm—make a tight fist.
2. Upper portion of the dominant arm—push your elbow down into the arm of the chair while simultaneously pulling your arm toward the torso.
3. Nondominant hand and forearm—same as with dominant hand and forearm.
4. Upper portion of the nondominant arm—same as above with dominant arm.
5. Forehead—arch your eyebrows as high as you can *or* knit your brows together.
6. Cheeks and nose—squint your eyes tightly while wrinkling your nose.
7. Jaws—clench your teeth together tightly while pulling back the corners of your mouth in an exaggerated smile.
8. Lips and tongue—with your teeth separated, press your lips together while pressing your tongue against the roof of your mouth.

9. Neck and throat—pull your chin down as if trying to touch it against your chest while simultaneously holding it back by counterposing the muscles involved, *or* (if you have a headrest) press your head back into the headrest.
10. Chest, shoulders, and upper back—after taking a deep breath, press your shoulder blades together behind you as if trying to touch them together.
11. Abdomen—after taking a deep breath, make the muscles of your stomach hard and taut, *or* make the muscles of your stomach tense by either pulling them in or pushing them out.
12. Thighs and upper legs—press your heels into the ground *or* press your knees together while at the same time trying to keep them apart by counterposing the muscles involved.
13. Calves—point your toes toward your head.
14. Feet—point your feet downward, while turning your feet inward and curling your toes under (remember to use about half as much pressure with the feet as with the other muscle groups).

Author Index

Subject Index

treatment studies, 29–31
very-low-calorie diet in, 56–58
Osteoarthritis. *See* Arthritis
Overeating,
  by bulimics, 6
Overweight, 2
Oxygen consumption, 9

Parotid gland, 14
Phenelzine sulphate, 68
Pondimin. *See* Fenfluramine
  hydrochloride
Potassium, 4
Prevalence
  of anorexia nervosa, 4
  of bulimia, 3, 11, 61
  of obesity, 4, 6
Problem
  identification, 48
  solving, 33, 45, 46, 49–51, 73, 87
  solving checklist, 121
Psychiatry, 97
Psychology, 97
Psychopathology, 74
Psychostimulants, 54
Psychotherapy, 32, 96, 101
  group, 32
  supportive, 101
Purging, 74

Questionnaire, 16

Reattribution, 104
Refundable deposit, 30
Reinforcement, 34, 45, 77, 90–91, 98
  conversation as, 91
  deprivation of, 91
  negative, 91, 99
  of weight gain, 98–99
Relapse
  identification of, 51–52
  in anorexia nervosa treatment, 103
  in bulimia treatment, 64, 87
  in obesity treatment, 51–52
  prevention, 73, 87–88, 90
Relaxation training, 81–83
Response prevention, 65–67, 81, 82

generalization of, 85
home practice of, 85
procedure, 83–85
rationale for, 82, 83
Responsivity
  external, 29

Salivary gland, 14
Salt
  light, 44
  reducing intake, 44
Self-disclosure, 72, 73, 76
Self-monitoring, 24–26, 34, 59, 68, 70,
    72, 79, 88
  and pharmacologic treatment, 68, 70
  computerized, 58–60
  forms, 26–27, 28, 40, 51–52
  resistance to, 79
Self-reward, 34
  in obesity treatment, 34, 45
Self-statements, 45
  changing, 45
Serum amylase, 14
Skills training, 32
Sleep apnea, 14
Snacking, 44, 55, 59
Social class, 2, 4
Social skills training, 95–96
Soft drinks, 42
Social environment, 44
  effects on eating, 44, 53
  in maintenance, 53
Sodium chloride, 44
Spices, 44
Spouse, 30
Starvation, 2
Statistical power, 90
Stimulus control, 29, 38, 43
Stress, 20, 82
  management of, 81–83
Suicide, 70

Temptation, 44
Thinking
  all or nothing, 74
  catastrophic, 104
Treatment

About the Author

W. **Stewart Agras**, professor of Psychiatry and Behavioral Science at Stanford University School of Medicine, received his MD from London University and completed his postgraduate training in psychiatry at McGill University. He is presently director of the Behavioral Medicine Program at Stanford, one of the first such programs in the country when it was founded in 1975. His research interests include both the study of eating disorders — anorexia nervosa, bulimia and obesity — and investigations into anxiety disorders, particularly focusing on agoraphobia. Much of the material for this book stems from his own research and clinical experience with the disorders of eating.

Dr. Agras was the first president of the Society of Behavioral Medicine and has also served as president of the Association for Advancement of Behavior Therapy. He is the only physician to hold both these positions. In addition to serving on many editorial boards, he was Editor for the *Journal of Applied Behavior Analysis,* has numerous publications in scientific journals, and is the author of three previous books.

After completing his postgraduate training at McGill he joined the faculty of the University of Vermont in 1961. Following this he became chairman of the Department of Psychiatry at the University of Mississippi Medical Center, leaving in 1973 to join the faculty at Stanford. He was also a Fellow at the Center for Advanced Studies in the Behavioral Sciences.